ANGELHEAD

ANGELHEAD

My Brother's Descent into Madness

Greg Bottoms

CROWN PUBLISHERS NEW YORK

Grateful acknowledgment is made to David Chernicky and *The Daily Press* for permission to reprint the following articles: "Suspect Called Sweet, Troubled . . ." by David Chernicky, Wednesday, April 15, 1992, page B3; "Years After Slaying, Man Surrenders" by Cheryl L. Reed, April 14, 1992, page A1; "Angry at Family, Man Sets Fire to Home . . ." by Matt Murray, February 24, 1993, page B1; "Poquoson Man Sentenced to 30 Years for Setting Fires . . ." by Mary Duan, November 24, 1993, page B3. Reprinted by permission.

Published by Crown Publishers, New York, New York.
Member of the Crown Publishing Group.

Random House, Inc. New York, Toronto, London, Sydney, Auckland
www.randomhouse.com

CROWN is a trademark and the Crown colophon is a registered trademark of Random House, Inc.

Printed in the United States of America

Design by Karen Minster

Library of Congress Cataloging-in-Publication Data
Bottoms, Greg.
    Angelhead : my brother's descent into madness / Greg Bottoms.—1st ed.
    1. Bottoms, Michael. 2. Schizophrenics—United States—Biography.
    3. Bottoms, Greg. 4. Schizophrenics—Family relationships. I. Title.
RC514.B593 B67   2000
616.89′82′0092—dc21
    [B]
                                                    000-021353

ISBN 0-609-60626-3

10 9 8 7 6 5 4 3 2 1

First Edition

Author's Note

This is a work of creative nonfiction. It is based upon the factual record of my brother's life, my own memory of the events described herein, and the anecdotes told to me that I am most inclined to believe. The whole, however, is held together by my imagination and is, to borrow a phrase from Michael Ondaatje, a literary "portrait or gesture" and not a history. In other words, its purpose—my purpose—is aesthetic as well as informative. My intention has been to capture the experience of schizophrenia. I hasten to add that I am not a mental health professional but quite simply a writer. Many of the names have been changed.

I think that faced with the mystery and

passion of life we are forced into a position

of humility that is best expressed in the

attitudes of prayer.

JOHN CHEEVER, *The Journals of John Cheever*

They ought to make it a binding clause

that if you find God you get to keep him.

PHILIP K. DICK, *Valis*

Contents

ANGELHEAD

GOD: A MEMORY

My brother saw the face of God. You never recover from a trauma like that. He was fourteen, on LSD, shouting for help in the darkness of his room in our new suburban home. I was ten. I stood watching from his doorway, still, eyes cinched up tight as seams, trying to make out his writhing shape. I saw for myself. I didn't see God, of course, but I saw my brother seeing God; I saw how petrified he was, how convinced. I knew, still know, that he saw, in some form, His or Her or Its face. It was in the window, a part of the night, shimmering over our neighborhood of new construction sites—clear plastic stapled to boards and waving in the night breeze, tire-tracked mud, portable toilets.

God in the lives of men is nothing new. It's a story that unfurls backward through the history of thought, meaning, reason. I've spent a lot of time tracing it, reading it over and over, in a hundred different ways. Characters change. There's a new setting, a twist in this plot that wasn't in that one. But it is an old, old story, as old as Story itself, and perhaps its beginning.

I compare my brother with other narratives involving God. God is the common language between us. That's how I place Michael, make sense of him, reimagine him—alongside saints and martyrs, lunatics and heretics, those who have fallen, shaken and supplicant, pleading, palms aimed heaven-ward, at the *thought* of God, His voice, the sweet, terrible whisper in their ear.

Jesus. Abraham, Jacob, Paul. Mark, Luke, Matthew, John. Joan of Arc, Hildegard of Bingen, John Brown. Charles Manson, Jim Jones, David Koresh.

Blake saw angels in trees. Thoreau imagined the possibility of divinity, the sublime, in a "knot-hole." Whitman saw God in the salivating mouth of a soldier's bullet hole. Mother Teresa knew the force of God lived even in the fecal rivers of Asian cities, the venereal fever of a beaten whore. I used to watch a man who lived on the streets of Richmond, Virginia, who spent hours shouting "Jesus" while in paroxysms, drool-ing, his fly open. But they didn't *see* Him. None of them. Not like my brother.

That night I couldn't move. The feeling of immobility, of being trapped, sticks in my mind. I stood in his doorway, a nightlight golden behind me, wearing pajamas, fat-faced and freckled, looking at my brother while he screamed, all open mouth and high-pitched wail. His face was contorted like a snake handler's, like a strychnine drinker's in the documentaries I would watch years later, late at night, with a VCR remote in my hand, slow-motioning the physical tics of madness.

I squinted into the darkness. Maybe, at ten, with my eyes barely open, I saw the future. Maybe I saw, in the dark of the room, heard in the screams, that one day soon he would be living on the streets, hungry; that he would be diagnosed as an acute paranoid schizophrenic; that he would leap from a van going forty-five miles per hour to avoid institutionalization; that he would frighten women, children, neighbors, us; that he would be raped; that he would admit to a murder he didn't commit; that his face would be on the front page of local newspapers, the killer; that he would attempt suicide for the first time by drinking Drano, the second time by hanging himself; that he would dismantle the fire alarms in my parents' home and set it on fire, ultimately ending up in the psychiatric ward of a Virginia maximum-security prison, praying and crying, by then all but dead to me, locked away in a place I would never visit, a brother—the same curve of flesh, angle of jaw, color of eyes—who had become a few cryptic Hallmark cards filled with biblical quotes.

I go over and over this. My memory is a scratched record. There I am, watching, cautious, afraid of him, afraid to step into the room because of his early propensity for petty cruelties: charley horses and wedgies, dirt clods and airplane spins, skinned knees and bloody lips and mean laughter. The stuff of early childhood, of brothers—but from him, different, darker, done with an eerie pleasure.

He ripped a poster from his wall, knocked over a red lava lamp, the only source of light within the room, spreading glass, a viscous gel.

My father built this house in the suburbs, most of it by himself. He could still barely afford it, had to sign half his life away to a bank. But we were away from blacks and crime and bad neighbors and people as poor as we were. We were pretending, for the sake of appearances, that we had money, though the old, rusty Rambler in our driveway must have given us away. Our pretending was in the scent of new wood, the chemical stench of fresh, shaggy carpets; it was in the long blades of light falling through our new windows from the streetlight outside, in my brother's screams.

It seemed plausible to me then that God could be in our window. I sometimes felt a cool tingle, like the breath of an invisible congregant, during the hymns at church. Electricity surged through me during sermons—the stained glass, the pastor's booming voice, the organ notes in my stomach and testicles. It was wonderful and frightening, the best and worst feeling. I've spent my life, starting from this moment in my brother's room, at once doubting and believing, fearing and embracing God—or at the very least the thought of God in me, the possibility of God, as George Steiner wrote, in some future tense made more of love than of hate. So I'm an atheist and a true believer. I value reason and hope for transcendence. I value the four strange, repetitive Gospels as much as any books I've read, but I can't imagine attending a church now, listening to simple aphorisms and affirmations, having become acutely suspect of all proclamations.

But I believed God was there for Michael that night, hovering in the window. I don't mean a hallucination; I'm not speaking figuratively; I mean that what was in the window that night for Michael was as real as the skin on his face. He'd stepped outside of our tenuous collective reality and into alternate space, a space where God was a shape, a newly decipherable language.

He had been at an Ozzy Osbourne concert at The Coliseum. It was 1980. He'd dropped six hits of acid. In his room he was having his first of many psychotic breaks. It came in the form of crippling guilt, ruthless introspection. He was Jesus being scolded by an angry Father. He wore sin, *all sin,* as heavy as lead shackles. God made him look at himself, and he was a stone with a minuscule heart.

He flailed. He cut his feet on the glass from the lava lamp. He turned and pleaded to and then punched a neon, glowing blacklight poster of Bruce Lee. God was torturing him with the things he had inside himself, with his own feelings and memories. His thoughts were razor-sharp. He started breaking everything he touched: piggybank in the shape of a football, spreading coins across the floor; his stereo case; a picture frame containing a family picture, each of us smiling under a blue sky against a blue blue ocean.

But memory fades, tricks, becomes convenient, reshapes itself. It's been nineteen years. I remember my mother and father there now, as if conjured from air or simple need, standing at the threshold of Michael's room. Glass scattered everywhere, shining like quartz.

My father hesitated. He wasn't much bigger than Michael, five feet eight inches, a hundred and sixty pounds. And Michael was swinging, the LSD pumping panic through his blood. My father knew. He wasn't surprised. He knew about the drugs and the heavy metal and the bad friends and the skipping school. Michael was a problem kid. Always had been. Foulmouthed. Willing to experiment with anything. My father knew and wanted to change things, to make it better, but the kid was out of control, sometimes violent. He knew how simultaneously sophisticated and irresponsible kids were these days. They knew more than they could handle knowing. They'd granted themselves a dangerous, cynical sort of freedom. Sex at twelve, thirteen. Drinking, drugs, even earlier. He knew. He even, if he would have thought hard enough about it, knew that mental illness was our family's sickness. His mother had been institutionalized. His own father, who was dead, had lived in a terminal funk, as if carrying the weight of a world that he knew cared nothing for him. His grandfather in North Carolina, a migrant worker, had clenched the barrel of a rifle between his teeth, spreading chunks of hair and bone and flesh along the wall, while his children were downstairs playing. Before this, my great-grandfather, as Michael would soon do, had taken to quoting scripture at length, mixing dogma with threats and expletives.

If my father had thought about it while watching Michael that night, he'd have realized that the chances of his son seeing the face of God, in some form, were not so astronomical, even without the acid.

I looked up at him—he seemed like a giant—wondering what was required of me. He wore sweatpants and a night-league softball shirt with "Three Dog Night" stenciled across the chest. He had big sideburns and wavy auburn hair, was only six or seven years older than I am now, with the massive hands of a worker. He was barefoot. It was after midnight, and the stars out the window were more ground glass.

What do I remember about my mother? She was composed. She was withdrawn. She must have been crying. She's always been given to quick, private tears. She knew Michael better than anyone, is perhaps the only person who has ever really *known* him, even though he hid things from her, was secretive to the extreme. In fact, this was the last straw in an ongoing line of last straws that spread out in front of us like taillights on a highway. This was the last straw like taking him back in the house after kicking him out will be the last straw, the last straw like picking him up from jail will be, the last straw, really, until the next last straw, and then the next. She was motionless, out in the hall, cast in shadow from the low-wattage nightlight.

These days she got calls from school, from neighbors, from the parents of girls her fourteen-year-old may have slept with. She got headaches she blamed on the stress of Michael. She prayed for Michael. She locked her bedroom door at night when my father wasn't home.

My father clicked on the light. That simple move seemed dangerous, bold, courageous. The room felt charged, alive. Shards of broken glass the size of human teeth spread over the floor. The lava lamp's snot glistened on the new carpet. Michael calmed. The window had now become a mirror. Instead of the accusatory face of God, the angry father, he saw only himself, a pallid face and tears and eyes black as coal.

His feet bled, were completely red with blood, glass sticking out of them in different directions like shark's teeth. My mother called for an ambulance. My father went to him, walking over the glass, not even considering the glass, and pulled him to his chest.

I remember my father—who died one month before Michael went to prison in 1993—sitting on the bed, holding Michael, this big kid in an Ozzy Osbourne T-shirt, sprawled awkwardly on his lap. They were rocking back and forth. Michael was slack, almost a corpse. He looked empty, drained of all life, of any former self.

I can see us all in my memory, even myself, the kid, the character, the narrator. It's quiet now. I smell the chemical newness of our home. I'm floating over my past to make it into a story. I have an aerial view: I see myself seeing the first evidence of my brother's blossoming insanity; I hear my first fragmented thoughts of God, feel my first real spiritual dread; I see my mother rummaging through the bathroom medicine cabinet for mercurochrome, Band-Aids; and I see my father— I see this most clearly—holding Michael, probably for the last time, holding him like an infant, shushing him, rubbing his hands through his sweaty hair. Their feet drip blood into a small puddle as if from one vein. My father is whispering. He is telling us it will all be fine.

From this false statement I begin.

MIDDLE-CLASS

I was a kid petrified of my odd and delinquent brother. I avoided him as much as possible. By all outward appearances, though, I was following in his footsteps. When I was twelve, I started growing up in wrong directions, creating my version of a punk artifice of nihilism to protect myself from the world. I wanted to hate things, but I didn't. I just pretended to. I was baffled by my life and home, baffled by my violent brother, unable to articulate, even to myself, why I was angry, why I was sad.

Once, when I was sent to the principal's office in the seventh grade for wearing a sleeveless T-shirt with a Heineken beer logo on the front, the vice-principal, an aging hippie who knew about my brother's drug

problems and all the fights he'd been in over the last few years
and his several brushes with the local police, asked me if I was
worried about nuclear war.

No, I said.

Is your family okay?

Yeah.

How about your brother Michael? Is he okay?

He's *great*.

You get along okay, then?

Sure, I said, we're close. I crossed my fingers to show
how close.

He paused. Does he ever . . . hurt you?

Nope.

Are you sure?

Yes.

Do you drink Heineken?

What?

But your brother does?

You're losing me now. I don't know what you're talking
about.

What kinds of music do you like?

I thought, Oh wow, you're really probing my mind now.
Stuff you can square dance to, I said.

Don't fuck with me, Greg.

I thought his saying "don't fuck with me" was amazingly
cool, so I told him the Dead Kennedys, the Circle Jerks,

Minor Threat, DRI, the Drunk Engines, Fear, the Germs, the Mekons—some of whom I had only heard mentioned by older skater kids I thought were far cooler than me.

Angry stuff, he said, that punk rock.

I guess.

Are you angry? he said. Are you scared of something? What worries you the most? Are you afraid . . . afraid that . . . you won't do well in life? Tell me about your family. I really want to know about you and your brother Michael.

Are we back to that? I said. I would rather have detention than talk about this shit again.

Don't use that language, he said.

You said "fuck."

You're twelve.

Detention it was. This was the drill: him pretending to be someone I should trust. I told him nothing but the name of a few bands. I would say anything to avoid talking about my brother. Truth is, I *wanted* detention. I wanted to tell my friends about my conversation with fuckwad the counselor. I *wanted* a *conflict* with *authority*. Thus a Heineken shirt without sleeves when I knew you had to have sleeves and could not wear beer or cigarette shirts or shirts with profanity or inappropriate messages to school. The shirt was my father's. He wore it to cut branches from trees and burn trash. It had stains all over it. Very punk. I had snuck back into my house to put it on when my mother thought I had gone to the bus stop that morning. My mother would never have let me wear that at twelve. I wanted a reason, even one I essentially created, to say fuck off to everything, my entire life and everybody in it. I used to get high and watch the punk classics *The Fall of Western Civilization* and *Rude Boy* over at my friend's house every weekend (Betamax tapes), and I wanted to be as careless and glamorously ruined as the people in those films.

There was an old woman in our neighborhood, a woman whom I referred to simply as "massive green hemorrhoid," for some reason, whose bright green yard I would often cut through. She told me one day as I jumped her fence, probably right into her beautiful hydrangea bushes, that I'd end up in prison just like my brother would. My English teacher that year told me I should take shop and learn a skill so I could make a living when I was older. That same teacher tried to have me expelled later when I wrote an A paper, insisting that I could not have done it, that I was not this smart, that I had actually copied the entire essay, word for word, out of a book. She knew of my family—especially knew of my brother—and it was impossible that I, this little punk asshole in the back of the class, could say anything of consequence about Stephen Crane. I found the whole thing flattering, and she ended up giving me an F on the paper and forgetting about the expulsion, which solidified my new punk philosophy perfectly because it made my underlying point about life: Do something the right way and still get the shaft.

I had already developed a taste for pot upon my introduction to it in the fifth grade. I liked the *easiness* of it when a friend of mine and I smoked some of his father's buds for the first time and watched one of his many pornos. We both sat, stoned out of our minds, with hard-ons and distressing looks on our faces and Oreo crumbs on our chins, unable to process the images on the screen. That year I started taking speed and diet pills. I drank alcohol, whenever I could get it, and Robitussin, which gives you a boozy, sleepy drunk. I skateboarded with my friends on ramps and on the road around gas stations and shopping centers and in empty pools. I stayed up all night watching endless hours of bad movies, stoned, until my memories, my life, started to feel like a pastiche of filmed clichés in which Michael occasionally made a cameo as the monster.

That year I shaved my head, wore giant rolled-up jeans, skater garb head to toe, and made straight Cs to prove something after years of nothing but straight As and honors classes. I started living, at twelve, as if yesterday were something I watched on TV. Tomorrow might not even come. This kind of nihilism was the essence of punk as I vaguely understood it, which, in many ways, was my one true, unwavering guide and mentor then, because my parents were always working to keep on top of their barely confinable debt, and when they weren't, they were dealing with a Michael crisis—a call from the cops or a teacher or a counselor or a parent. There was always something. I was free.

My father was always working on the house—making a flower bed, painting something, hammering, sawing. It was his pride and joy; he couldn't believe we actually lived in it.

My mother and younger brother, Ron, who was seven, hovered in their own little worlds made of clubs, homework, sports, and spelling bees. My mother doted on Ron and me, kissing us, hugging us without warning, telling us at least twice a day, at breakfast and when she got home late from work, how much she loved us, how special we were. But she avoided close contact with Michael even then, because there was something dangerous about the vibrations he seemed to give off, the way he could turn on you and start screaming and cursing without warning.

We didn't understand him, had no idea he was getting sick, mentally and spiritually, with a horrible disease. With sympathy, the early stages of schizophrenia are a massive burden; without sympathy and understanding, without love and care even in the face of the strangest of behaviors, schizophrenia is a wrecking ball.

My father, unlike my mother, almost never gave away his emotions, except for the anger he directed at Michael. He was embarrassed by his feelings. He had grown up in a home without love, filled with petty cruelties and alcoholism and despair, a place where dreams of a better life were absurd and worthy of venomous critique from his own father.

Once my father and I, about this time, were wrestling in the den and laughing before a Redskins game. My father loved me, I know, but his love was precarious, volatile at times. To express love openly is to leave yourself open to injury, which he could not take, not even slightly. He rubbed his coarse beard on my face. It was a joke, a tiny torment in a game of joking torment—boy play, my mother called it—but it burned my skin and I became angry. Then he laid all his weight on me and I couldn't breathe. He stayed like that for a minute or more, even though I was panicking. He rolled over and poked me in the side with his finger, a little too hard, breathing heavy and smiling. He didn't know how strong he was, how he had nearly crushed me, how the lightest brush from his face had nearly ripped my skin. Lying beside me, he looked me in the face and said he loved me. He made as if to hug me.

I told him I hated him.

His face blanked with rage, became colored with a whole history of tiny failures and rejections. Something inside him turned. He got to his knees and began smashing his open hands against my face and ears. I curled up in a knot to weather the blows. My mother came into the room screaming. That was enough to stop my father. He stood up, face red, hair a mess, and, pointing down at me on the floor, he said he hated me. Well *I* hate *him* too. He spoke like a ten-year-old and it scared me.

I wasn't physically hurt, but there was a gaping hole in my chest from having my father tell me he *hated* me, even after I had told him first. I felt I could say it with impunity, but not him; if he could say he hated me back—and at that moment, looking at him, I *knew* that he meant it more than I did—then he wasn't really my father. I went down to a friend's house— his divorced father was never home—and smoked more dope, ate Oreos, drank a few beers, and watched porno.

—

Michael never fully came back after the Ozzy Osbourne concert, the six hits of acid, the seeing God. He was out of sync with the rest of the world, a giggling, scowling acidhead. He pulled strange stunts: setting small fires in surrounding neighborhoods, telling teachers he had testicular cancer, grabbing his crotch, twisting his scrotum up in his hand in front of the class, smirking; shooting BBs at neighborhood kids; tossing me into fresh-cut poison ivy and laughing at the weeping sores I'd have later that night, my swollen eyes and fingers.

He was famous in our new town of ten thousand white people as the good-looking bad boy. He resembled a muscular Keifer Sutherland (of *Young Guns* as opposed to *Flatliners*)—long blond hair, blue eyes, lanky but fit. He would take any drug, drink until he was facedown in some kid's suburban living room. But he still had one foot in reality at this point. His strangeness was attributed to the drugs my parents knew he did; he was an eccentric from a family tree full of eccentrics, a violent kid from a family in which violence, like alcoholism, ran in our blood, trickled down. Much of my father's family was famously, tragically damaged, stretching back generations, from the farms of North Carolina and my great-grandfather's macabre exit, to rural Appalachia, back across the Atlantic to Scotland and Ireland: alcohol, depression, manic-depression, suicide. You had to figure, statistically, that at least one of us would bump up against some dread so great that he'd lose his mind.

But the suburbs were treating us well at this time, which made our problems—my illicit drug use at twelve, my brother's rather open drug use and declining mental state—seem distant, not worth dwelling on. Big colonial homes sat on plush green cul-de-sacs. Fog patches floated above us in the morning like fat gray whales. You could smell the salt air of the Chesapeake Bay from our house. Sprinklers. Dogs barking. Neighborhood picnics. Baseball. County fairs. This was the America my father had always yearned for, and on the surface it was as beautiful and peaceful as his dreams of it had been.

Before we had moved away from our old neighborhood in Hampton, Virginia, my mother had been a school-bus driver in one of the worst sections of the city, Pine Chapel, a HUD housing development of barracklike structures. I remember riding in the seat behind hers, remember the black kids talking about the white bitch and her kid, how she drove and never said anything. Pine Chapel was all black, and the poverty and violence these people lived in was mind-numbing. There were knife fights and muggings and racial beatings and shootings. My father, because of the stories my mother told him, because of her fear, because of where we lived and the public schools we went to, became a secretive racist just as his father had been an open one. So these white suburbs were a symbol of success to him. A grand white success. He cut branches. He burned trash. He swept and edged the sidewalk.

My parents had new friends now, friends with *money*, pools, big houses, expensive cars, golf and traveling and drinking habits. They had to adjust their way of thinking, to learn to not let their faces show surprise when a Rolex was worn to a party, or a giant diamond hung around an alabaster neck, or when someone invited them onto a massive luxury fishing boat for the day. They had to learn to be blasé around copious, conspicuous cash, and to act as if they, somehow, had their own large stash.

My father began wearing khakis and boat shoes and Izod shirts, relegating his uniform of Redskins jerseys, Chuck Taylors, and Levi's to yard-work status. This was their dream— this place among the marginally wealthy, two-car garage, kids-go-to-college set.

My father longed to belong in a group of people for whom winning—and that's what this was, the conventional American definition of winning—was not alien and unattainable. He was embarrassed about where he came from, that he had quit high school and then gone back and barely finished years later, that he had never set foot on a college campus. People could look at my parents, their house, their clothes, and my parents were unashamed, making it by all outward appearances.

They were happy these days, in love, as long as Michael wasn't somehow ruining it for them, wasn't bleeping across a police scanner or getting expelled from school or mildly overdosing in some kid's upstairs bathroom. They bought a huge Zenith TV, trinkets for the house, flowers that bushed up around our foundation, giving off the fragrance of middle-class normalcy.

But Michael's state of mind was sinking fast. I can see that, looking back, though at the time none of what makes perfect sense now made any sense at all. We all had our mechanism for pretending otherwise: my modes of escape and general punk attitude; my father's single-minded quest for conventional success; my mother's relentlessly positive attitude; my younger brother Ron's youth and lack of understanding.

Michael was confused and confined, stuck in murky thoughts of God and demons, already uttering odd fragments of church-speak, dialogue from horror flicks, and lyrics from heavy metal. Every day he seemed more outrageous, more defiant. Mumblings. A vague panic. People plotting against him.

At first, when he heard the voices after seeing God's face, it was like everything opened up for him, like the world made sense for the first time. The colors were brighter, the sounds were sharper. Narratives arose, beautiful, intricate narratives, where none had existed before. Everything could be connected. The most trivial things seemed vital. But now things were getting darker.

All of Michael's friends were still in Hampton, the next city over, in our old neighborhood. He didn't like the kids with money, had trouble making new friends with schizophrenia blooming in his brain, with this school full of strangers he was convinced whispered about him behind his back.

Michael's world started breaking into tiny pieces. He laughed for no reason, nowhere near a punchline. He said off-color things about death and dying and torture, about corpses and axes and Satan. He would look at a clock to tell the time, but then he'd see the round frame, the glass, the hands red and black, one sweeping, one still, and the actual calculation of time suddenly escaped him, moved just out of reach of his thoughts. Everything was like this. The world was like this.

At first it was perfect, this breakdown in thinking, this shattering of meaning, the perfect trip, the permanent high, but then he was stuck. He couldn't get out of his head. He couldn't say what he meant. Words got jumbled. Meaning was a series of knots. He became angry and depressed, buzzed with a kind of low-wattage rage.

Many of Michael's friends, those kids from Hampton who had grown into their teens with police records, had cars—Novas, Mustangs, El Caminos. They drove the thirty minutes to pick him up for the weekend, never getting out of the car, just beeping in the driveway, engine rumbling, windows smoked over, choking gas fumes bellowing out of the rusty exhaust pipe. They listened to Black Sabbath and Iron

Maiden and Motley Crüe—a particularly delinquent group of kids who were so high all the time they barely noticed any change in my brother.

My mother would peek out the window as Michael ran out the door saying he was staying with one friend or another. For a while my father tried to stop him. The fights they had over this when Michael would return on Sundays sometimes lasted hours and usually ended up in a house full of tears and overturned furniture, another Sunday night melee. I'd crank up the stereo or the TV or both to drown out the yelling, the crashing.

My father would use a fat leather belt to beat Michael. The thwacks sounded like the punches and kicks in martial-arts films. I've always had an aversion to violence—it can make me physically ill. I've thrown maybe three punches in my entire life, which is odd for a boy who ran in the crowds I ran in. I trace my fear, my learned ability for compromise in moments of conflict, my outright—here's the truth— *cowardice* in the face of real violence, back to the solid sounds of those blows on my brother's back and head and legs.

After the beatings, my father would often go into the backyard and pretend to do yard work. He'd try to talk himself away from the act, from the uncontrollable anger that made him swing and swing. He would sometimes cry if he'd really hurt Michael, if there were bruises, but that wouldn't stop him the next time, because he didn't know how else to handle a kid like Michael, a kid, he knew, who was heading straight for prison or the grave. He thought if he'd acted like that, his father would simply have killed him.

At some point, worn down and worn out, my father gave up on trying to stop Michael from hanging out with kids he knew sold and took drugs, the same kids with whom Michael had taken six hits of acid at one time.

My father was exhausted when it came to Michael. He had worked so hard to get here, to get to this suburb. He had this new life where everything but his family looked promising.

SACRIFICE

The city where my family lived from 1965, five years before I was born, to late 1977 was built around shipbuilding and fishing. Hampton is less than thirty miles from Jamestown, Yorktown, and Williamsburg, three of America's first settlements and beacons of historical tourism. Oddly, everything in Hampton looks as if it were built in the late 1930s and early 1940s, when the big business of Military took over, when the Tidewater area was deemed a "strategically sound location." Since then the military has dwindled, though there are still several bases—army, navy, air force, marine—nearby, and there has always been, at least to me, a transient, characterless feel to the place.

To the south, across the wide mouth of the James River, where it empties into the Chesapeake Bay, is Norfolk and Virginia Beach, bridges and hotels and All-U-Can-Eat seafood buffets and T-shirt outlets and boat shows. To the east is Chesapeake Bay and then the rural, insect-infested Eastern Shore, that thin strip of land with its crab pots and peanut fields, farm equipment, fruit stands, and beautiful old homes. Beyond that, the dark Atlantic.

They are rebuilding Hampton nowadays, making it into a place for young professionals, with nice restaurants and beachfront properties going up where once only slums were (the slums have moved a few blocks and been condensed and are now more heavily patrolled by city police); nightclubs thrive; the parks are full of couples and families every weekend.

In 1983, however, when a young boy I will call S was murdered in our old neighborhood, Hampton was a place from which people wanted to move. It had been in steady economic and aesthetic decline since the early sixties. The buildings of downtown went unrented; they had cracked mortar and broken windows and some had begun to lean with their shadows toward the empty, trash-filled streets. The lower-middle-class suburban neighborhoods were racially mixed and volatile. The schools were among the worst in the state.

Here, just a few miles from where my father had attended high school and quit and attended again, just a few miles from our old house, my brother and his friends had a fort in the thick forest between the Briar Queen public pool and our old neighborhood. The fort sat deep in the guts of these woods, the same woods where I used to play after school when I was six and seven.

On the edge of the woods, half a mile from my brother's fort, there was a black man, a Vietnam vet, living on top of the junior high school, a man smelling of urine and feces and garbage, dressed in rags, a hat made of newspaper. His face was covered in fat, light brown scars like slugs. The neighborhood legend was that he had been a POW. He made toy birds out of leaves and pinecones. He spoke a kind of Southern urban gibberish, shouting from the roof to the kids below about the merits of calisthenics, the nutritional value of army rations.

From 1977 to 1983 my brother went regularly with friends to loiter around the junior high. They got drunk on bag-wrapped quarts of beer and stoned on ditch-weed joints, laughed, threw dirt clods, aiming for faces, for mouths and eyes. Sometimes they slugged it out with rival basketball teams, friend or foe, didn't matter who, just something to do. They either walked there from their fort or drove a guy named Clyde's VW bug, all of them packed in like clowns in a clown car, pot smoke billowing out of windows, bass beats bouncing off houses and into the sky.

They had to jump a high fence to come and go at the school after hours. Graffiti covered the building's bland concrete walls—gang insignia (B-Section Boys), or terse commands

(Suck Me). They shot hoops on the outside courts—steel nets stuck to bent rims—and acted as obnoxious as bullies do anywhere.

For fun, for something to do, they called the old man on the roof a coon, a jigaboo, a spook, a spear-chucker. They said, nigga pleeze, said, yo, wipe that fuckin slug off yo face, nigga.

From the roof, the old man, covered in dirt from being recently hit with a dirt clod, told them again, this time with tears in his eyes, to do calisthenics or perish in physical disrepair.

—

It was here, on June 10, 1983, just a few hundred yards from Michael and his friends' fort, just down the road from the junior high and the homeless black veteran on the school roof, that S was murdered. I believe I would have all but forgotten the murder by now, wouldn't have to imagine and reimagine it, if it hadn't later become central to the story of my brother.

I picture a boring late afternoon in our old rundown neighborhood in our old rundown city, picture the small brick homes lined up straight as tombstones.

All the kids are inside watching TV as usual, *Batman* and *Romper Room*. They're lounging around on the shag carpets of their homes, mothers in kitchens, talking on phones, twisting cords around fingers, smoking cigarettes at kitchen tables, having kicked off one of those furry slippers to scratch their calves absentmindedly with their painted toenails.

Houses sit quietly. There's a siesta-like hush. Cars inch by on the streets, rolling through stop signs. Music in the distance. Someone washing a car. The tops of trees in the woods sway softly.

S—who is thirteen and quiet and a star student at an increasingly dangerous school—is heading to a friend's house on the other side of the woods, in Powhatan Park. He walks into the woods, shade falling like a curtain, then stops. He starts turning over logs, looking for bugs for a science project that his father, who has high hopes for S, has promised to help him with. He's wearing shorts and sneakers, thick glasses. He's skinny, clumsy, and trips over a stump, stumbling forward.

It's warm and gray, wind blowing in from the nearby Chesapeake. Green leaves and branches on the ground, across the path. The world is empty, desolate. The world is his.

He could spend all day out here on an empty afternoon like this, looking at bugs and spores, moss and mushrooms and fungi.

He opens his fly, pisses. He is smiling, pissing in the empty woods, pissing on a *natural habitat* full of *specimens*. He zips up, but slowly, unconcerned, convinced he's alone.

He digs a hole, sifts earth through his fingers, looking for life, feeling the coolness in his hands. He hears something, looks around, nothing. He sighs, leans against a tree, looks up at the tree tops, branches dividing the sky. He takes off his glasses, rubs his eyes—everything blurs.

A gang of boys ride up on bikes, white kids he doesn't know, has never seen, like a pack of ghosts, out of nowhere. They're filthy, spotted in dirt, holes in their clothes, some kind of lower-middle-class urban horde. They say, *Look ahere,* say, *What the fuck,* say, *Ho-ly ssshhhit.* There are ten, twelve of them.

Or he does know them, knows them well. They surround him. *Come on,* he says, palms up, pleading with half a smile bending his face.

It's some older kids—seventeen, eighteen years old, maybe drug dealers, a satanic cult (a popular notion since *Rosemary's Baby, The Exorcist, Carrie,* and *The Omen* have made their way to *The ABC Saturday Night Movie*). They look dead, these kids, look like zombies, skeletal shadows in trenchcoats.

They ride up on motorcycles, but he doesn't hear them until the engines are whining loudly, nasally, beside him.

A group of black kids walk up, quietly, ducking behind trees until they snatch him by the arms. Black kids from the projects a half-mile away.

Or it's some of those Vietnamese—or are they Cambodian?—immigrants that work for minimum wage at the seafood docks downtown. Those people are nuts, S knows, scared of everything, scared of America, driving their boats up on sandbars because they don't understand the English channel markers, talking that gibberish my father mimicked, *Heyro, you wan scarrops or free, four fish.* They have orange-handled fish-gutting knives. Someone told him they eat dog.

No. One man, white, slender, a pedophile. He walks up, a serial killer spending one single day in the city. It is just terrible luck straight out of a movie.

He has a mustache, a beard, is clean-shaven. He has long hair, is balding, is going gray. He's wearing a coat, a T-shirt with something written on the front, he's bare-chested, all hair and big pink nipples.

It is the black man, the exercise guy, who lives on top of the school. He's hunting children in the late-afternoon warmth. His mental impairments have affected his frontal lobe and thus his moral judgment. Perhaps his brain will one day make it into the hands of science. He bets S he can do more push-ups. *You go first,* he suggests.

It is my brother and his friends, just screwing around, and something, something really awful and accidental, happens.

It is my brother out in the woods, by himself, still hearing those first, faint voices, the world a bright, glowing puzzle that has begun to make him angry. He hears God or Satan ticking off something in Morse code, using branches and wind.

S doesn't see them coming. The guy is just there. He sees him coming, but he doesn't look threatening.

The guy looks hurt. Looks helpless. Looks angry, sad, sick.

He limps, runs, walks and whistles. He says he's feeling sick.

He knows him. The guy waves, smiles, says, *Could you help me, son?*

He is overdressed, almost naked, doing something in the woods by himself.

He lives down the street. He hangs out at the pool.

Or: Maybe they've been meeting for weeks, months.

Are you doing some kind of class project? he says. *I'm a friend of your dad's. Your mom sent me. How many push-ups can you do? What are you so afraid of?*

S puts on his glasses, leans hard against that tree, looking up at the branches caging the sky, and next thing, *wham* . . .

S is looking down into a hole, at termite larvae wriggling around wet roots, and someone taps him on the shoulder.

S is tying his shoe and then is on his stomach, a knee in his back, something tight around his neck.

They slam him against a tree.

They throw him down, hard.

He takes off his belt, unzips his pants.

He lifts a thick branch to shatter his skull.

He is smiling, then, suddenly, gripping S's face like a bowling ball.

He puts a funny-smelling handkerchief over S's mouth. It tastes like metal, it tastes like salt.

He doesn't give a fuck so everything is possible, and killing is just part of his day.

S struggles like a champ.

He gives up.

He pleads, cries.

He is just sort of blank.

He never knows what hit him.

The guy is touching himself, but everything is okay, then the guy starts talking about his dick, talking about his dick like it's another person standing here, with an opinion, with a temper. *Look,* he says. *Look,* like S did something to him that now he has to pay for.

Before S is unconscious, he sees a tree, the ground, the blurry shape of his glasses on summer leaves, a white face, a black face, an old face, a young face, a strange face, a familiar face, a bunch of faces looking down at him, edgeless and coagulating; a face from the TV, my brother's face; he sees a knee, a bare foot, a boot, a tennis shoe, white; he sees a blur of green and brown because the guy is swinging him around by his neck and he is vanishing into a dream already.

He just watches as his own sock moves over his face and tightens around his neck; he sees his killer(s), but he is already dead and won't be answering any questions.

He sees himself from above and thinks, *God, I'm just a kid. What kind of world is this?*

He doesn't believe this moment is real. And maybe it's not.

He is reborn in the light of God.

He doesn't feel anything anymore. He's a body without a soul, or without the chemical synapses required to be considered alive. However you want to define it. Whatever you want to believe. He's just dead. The instant came and he was no longer.

—

A search party gathered early the next morning. S's family must have been frantic. But you never expect the worst. You can't. You'll lose your mind expecting the worst.

Men spread out and marched through the woods. Flashlight beams pierced the dawn. Within an hour, there was a body. No dramatic complication, no Movie of the Week, nothing of the sort. They started looking and there it—he—was.

The cops came, worked on the crime scene through the day, June 11, 1983.

S had been strangled by his own left sock and raped. There was evidence—blood, skin, semen. It was a reckless crime, unplanned, a crime of passion. It made the front page of the local paper the next morning, below the fold. I read it sitting at my kitchen table. S was one year older than me. I watched it on the six o'clock news. I said to myself, I know this person, but didn't feel anything. I tried to will myself to feel something. It was just words on a page, a pretty anchorwoman perfunctorily reciting a story. Another dead kid.

—

Once the body had been carted away in a black bag, my brother and his friends got as close as they could to the crime scene the next morning. My mother later told me that

Michael said he was going to solve the crime and collect the reward. He told her about the black man on the school roof.

I wonder now what my brother, at seventeen, was thinking as he looked at the chalk-drawn shape of a body in the dirt. Did he feel guilt, even then, or was it only later, when the voices were chattering accusations, when the conspiracy against him was complex beyond explanation, drowning out everything?

My father, after a long search, found Michael at the edge of the woods where the body was found. He was alone and dazed. It was close to dusk of the same day, the day after the murder. My father, frantic, after calling around for Michael for hours, had driven down here in our Rambler. Michael hadn't been home in two days. No one had seen him since that morning. None of his friends knew where he was. He was in the woods, they said, but then he said he was going home, that my mother was going to pick him up.

In the car, my father told Michael he was never coming back here, never hanging out with those guys again if he expected to live at home.

Do you hear me?

Michael, filthy now after going a few days without a shower, looked out the window, out at the blurred world. Black clouds sailed over a dying sunset and he could feel a storm coming. When he closed his eyes, he could hear the dead boy whining, could see the tears streaming down his face as he tried to scream.

—

The cops questioned more than two hundred people around those neighborhoods, black and white. They went door to door. They talked to all of my brother's friends. They didn't talk to Michael because he was living in a new town now and somehow his name never came up.

All the kids—all my brother's friends—said it was the vet on top of the school. They decided to murder him—*to kill the nigger*—but he was already gone: vanished without a trace. Michael, however, knew the vet didn't do it. God, impersonating a tree in the woods, told him so.

SECRETS

In our new city, lawns were cut, cars washed.
Piano lessons were given, the school band
practiced on the football field, baseball season played toward the series championships.
People die every day. S was just another
dead kid. He barely made it through a news
cycle.

Michael slowly slipped further and further away, deeper and deeper into the early
stages of madness. He began spending more
time alone with the snakes he collected. He
kept them as pets and built elaborate aquarium habitats for them in his room. (He had
gone through a tarantula phase, too, but
something had malfunctioned with the halo-
gen light in his aquarium and fried both of

his spiders into hairy clenched fists. Thank God he didn't replace them.)

He liked the snakes' smooth, perfectly patterned skin, their liquid movements, the soft, cautious flicker of the tongue. He liked the way snakes *sensed* the dangers of the world, the dangers he himself had begun to sense. He liked, also, that people were frightened of snakes, and sometimes, even though he knew it was wrong, he savored the look of fear on a person's face when confronted by them.

He would watch the snakes eat large mice for hours with his lights down low. As the shiny skin bulged around the snake's throat, the mouse stuck momentarily, wriggling, still alive, a life absorbing another—a fact of nature, he liked to say, smiling—he wondered what that felt like, absorbing another's life, taking its spirit. He believed he could absorb life-forms through his skin.

At night, when he was seventeen, he dreamed the snakes spoke to him in their secret language, a language of pure sense, a language without words.

He felt confused these days, once he knew he was outside of his dreams. People—teachers, my mother, his last few remaining friends—would talk to him but then their words would get lost before they reached his mind; it was as if the words would sometimes get caught up in the air, as if the air were heavy, almost solid, and the words, like hard objects, fell to the ground before they reached him. Other times, when the words did reach him, each word was wearing a disguise, each word actually contained the meanings of many words and how was he to know, how the fuck was he to know, if he could trust the legitimacy, the *honesty,* of this word?

But the snakes made sense. Sometimes he was afraid to leave his room and the snakes because an engulfing light was probably in the hall waiting for him. It might be the light of God, sure, but if it wasn't—then what?

And there were the times when he wanted to know something, study it, but then he couldn't, for the life of him, remember what it was. It—this wordless feeling he associated with his earlier vision of God in our window—vanished when he reached out his hand. The pain from this was almost physical. The world was a trick, a hall of mirrors, and he couldn't tell whether he was even himself sometimes or whether he was simply *a reflection* of himself, one of those reflections that had been sent out in quadruplicate from the center, the actual Michael, which he may not have ever been. Sometimes he cried and he couldn't remember why he'd started.

He felt, at other times, as if he were dead. He wanted to rise again but couldn't unravel the riddle of resurrection, of how to save yourself. He started checking out books on the occult from the local library, smuggling them into the house under his jacket.

He seemed to think that the snakes were a key to unlocking the mystery of this crisis of meaning. They comforted, kept beautiful secrets he could almost decipher when his eyes were closed. He read that snakes were a symbolic representation of sin, death, evil, temptation, sex.

Whenever I encountered him, he would stare at me until I walked out of a room, my heart pounding, a permanent frown on his face. Michael kept to himself—hunched, lonely, looking over his shoulder always. I thought of him as dangerous, someone to lock the door against.

The condition known as schizophrenia was named by the German psychiatrist Eugen Bleuler in 1911. The term denotes a splitting of the various parts of the thought process. It does not make a person evil, or even necessarily dangerous. Some theories posit that schizophrenia does not actually change underlying personality traits: once affected, people who worry will continue to worry, people with a good sense of humor will continue to have one, a laid-back person will continue to be so, and so forth.

Schizophrenics can become dangerous, though, through lack of care, which leads them into desperation, and most especially through a lack of understanding and sympathy, which was, obviously and accidentally, the case in my home.

Evil is a tougher question, but in my brother's case I believe it was his nature. When he wasn't sad or hurt or lonely, Michael was the meanest person I have ever known. His petty ruthlessness when we were boys seemed almost limitless.

Once, when I was ten or eleven and Michael was fourteen or fifteen, a neighborhood bully a few years older than me smashed me over the head with a metal-bottomed motorcycle seat. It knocked me almost unconscious. When I regained my senses, Michael had blackened both of the bully's eyes, burst his nose into a torrent of bright red blood, and made him eat dog shit. I started crying. I felt sick from all the blood on the concrete, the lump on my head, and I told my brother to stop, to not make him eat that, that it was okay and I was fine and it had been an accident, just a dumb accident. He told me to shut the fuck up or I would eat the dog shit, too. He handed me a rock and made the kid get on his knees with his hands behind his head and his face presented to me. I made a bloody divot in his forehead the size of a dime. We left him lying in his front yard. Michael told me that if I looked over my shoulder at him I was dead.

——

After reading about snakes, he wondered if they were trying to trick him. Were they really connected to the one true God, or were they merely false messengers, like the one in Genesis? He couldn't know for sure. He was still held in by his mortality. He was trying, through dreams and prayer, to devise a way to step fully outside of this realm, the realm of the body, into the purely spiritual. He knew the world would be laid waste soon, and a recommunion with God seemed necessary yet impossible and frustrating.

He knew that if he told anyone in the waking world about his dreams, about the language of snakes—and sometimes he wanted to tell my mother, because he loved my mother, though he made her life nearly unbearable for twenty-six years—they'd think he was crazy, think his mind was full of cracks and fissures.

There were three snakes: a king snake, black with white stripes; a rat snake, brown, mottled, big-headed, small-eyed; and a black snake he'd found in the copse behind our home, wet-looking, as dark as coal. He would often sit in a lawn chair in the backyard, with a snake in each hand, coiled up around each arm. He would kiss them on the thin mouth, talk to them in whispers, while I stared out the back window.

My parents didn't like the snakes, of course, but thought a hobby, even this hobby, was good for Michael. They imagined him, fueled by a new interest in science, biology, zoology, straightening up. They didn't realize then that what the snakes represented to him was metaphysics, the hidden meaning of good and evil through a better understanding of the occult. To them, anything, even large live snakes in the house, was better than drugs, dark moods, violent impulses, family fights. Not that any of these things subsided. But they hoped.

Each night during that year, the year of the murder, he locked himself away in his room, listened to Pink Floyd, Led Zeppelin, Black Sabbath, letting the snakes, all three, crawl over his nude body, slither around his face and neck, legs and groin. Their cool, rubbery touch gave him strength, spiritual strength, to unravel his dreams, but still it was never quite enough. Nothing was enough, and it made him angry. There was something to *know,* some vast plain of knowledge just out of reach. The frustration of not knowing made his mood swings monstrous, every second in his presence volatile.

We avoided him; he avoided us. The house became more and more somber. There were moments of happiness, few and far between, and always when Michael was elsewhere and it was just my mother, my father, Ron, and me, but home life as Michael got sicker and more paranoid was dusty and melancholic and claustrophobic.

It was when I went to friends' homes, sat around their dinner tables talking about school, about football, about girls and current events and movies, even telling jokes, that I realized how strange my home life was.

Occasionally, when friends of mine came over, we'd spend afternoons looking out the window at Michael with snakes coiled around him in the backyard. I once charged a dollar each for a group of five boys to look out my window at my brother talking to his snakes.

Man, one said, I can't believe they haven't locked his ass *up.*

PENANCE

Michael was a black belt in karate. Despite the voices and the depression and the anger, he'd been studying martial arts twice a week at a local dojo for three years, since he was fifteen, and he excelled.

He had always been a great athlete; built like a big gymnast, he had, in the last few years, become fanatical about the martial arts and lifting weights in the same way he had become fanatical about God, reading the Bible, studying the occult, and trying to listen to the messages of the snakes.

His athletic ability was amazing: he could jump up, kick the hanging light fixture in our kitchen, a good seven feet high, softly enough so that it didn't even move, snapping his leg back at the last second; he could drop, instantly, into a split; he could spin in the air, wheeling one hard, weaponlike foot around in a flesh-colored blur.

Michael and a neighbor, Bill, who took karate with Michael on Wednesday nights and was one of his last remaining friends, had discovered the potent combination of speed and working out. They were getting to be—according to me, a kid who also dabbled in speed—speed freaks. They took pills with absurd names: blue torpedoes, white crosses, black beauties, sometimes got their hands on a line or two of crystal meth.

Michael loved speed because it amped his nerves, which he thought was good for both karate workouts and listening for God. Like a ninja, he could hear the sneezes of rodents, the steps of a grasshopper; he could hear angels in trees and raindrops bubbling in the ripped-apart clouds above. If he took enough, he could hear his spine vibrate like a struck triangle, sending a steady harmony down to those weapon-like feet.

We were latchkey delinquents, my brother and I, our parents doing all they could to keep ahead of their debt. The house was almost always empty of adults. But the only real danger my brother and I faced in our suburb, a place with virtually no serious crime, was ourselves. My younger brother spent his afternoons at an overpriced local day-care center for kids aged five to twelve.

In our garage, after school, Michael and Bill sometimes whaled on a punching bag chained to a wooden ceiling beam.

They would get revved up on pills, fling sweat all over the place, shout, the chain ringing and clinking.

Bill was a brown belt, but lanky, weak, and less coordinated than Michael. My brother, on the other hand, looked like some Caucasian version of Bruce Lee, his hero, all sinewy muscles, striations, full of long, complicated silences. Michael was smart enough to keep his grander delusions to himself, to guard his secret life from his friends and family, and this, certainly, had a lot to do with how quiet he became.

One day, a year or so after the murder of S, I was in my room sketching, my artistic outlet back then. I was coming off a lunchtime high—a good time to sketch. My brother was out cutting the grass, a dictate from my father—it had to be cut by the time he got home.

Most days I went to a guy named Kirk's house, who was fifteen but looked thirty, whose college-age brother sold cocaine and had a propensity for high-speed, somehow survivable, car crashes. Years later, Kirk lost everything and then went into rehab and found God. He got a girl pregnant after that and married her to do the right thing without considering how much he secretly hated her. But back then he had these parties every day after school because his parents traveled for weeks at a time on business—actually, there was just kind of an ongoing party at Kirk's house, a kind of puking, fucking, teenage bacchanal. I shot pool and drank cheap beer and smoked weak pot. You could hear kids creaking the beds upstairs sometimes, usually the football players and their girlfriends. Evidently there were some layovers, some business deals gone bad, and now Kirk's dad was home for the week and I didn't have anything to do but go home and sketch myself down from a high.

So I was at home, upstairs, nothing to smoke, nothing to drink, nothing to do: door closed, a breeze blowing the curtains in, the smell of freshly mown grass, the voices of kids shouting in the distance. The lawnmower engine sputtered, stopped. I was lost in what I was working on. So it took a few seconds, or maybe minutes, for me to notice the silence, look up.

When I looked up, Michael and Bill were standing over me, Bill grinning, Michael blank-faced, empty-eyed. I tried to look nonchalant, like I was ready to ignore them. I said, in a half-whisper, What's up? I felt my heart beat in my throat and temples.

What the fuck are you *drawing*? said Bill over my left shoulder (usually I drew surreal, menacing-looking landscapes).

Go cut the grass, Michael said, deadpan. Me and Bill got stuff to do.

I said, calmly, it was his turn this week, feeling tired and distant from the pot I'd smoked earlier.

They wanted me to answer this way. It was in their smiles. This wasn't about grass-cutting. It was about karate. They took an arm each, then floated down the stairs, out the sliding patio door, into the yard—tall green grass, high wood fence, trees, long fat shadows.

Start the lawnmower.

Fuck you.

Bill laughed, said, *Oooh myyy God.*

Michael clenched his fists, as if this were the cue to begin, assumed his karate stance. Start the mower, motherfucker, or I'm going to kill you.

Fuck you, I said. I smelled fresh-cut grass. The sun was burning hot, the heat dry. Everything was green. I tried to smile, to break the tension.

The first kick stunned me, landing in the center of my chest, my ribs giving under it.

Start the mower. Or I will *kill* you.

I was on the ground now, on my hands and knees, and I couldn't breathe. I got up, world hazy at the edges, and started walking toward the house. I was afraid to fight, especially my brother, who towered over me with his strength like a God at that time. The house wobbled, tilted, leaned, moved away.

Next came a swing-around foot sweep. Right out of *Enter the Dragon,* a movie my brother had seen at least thirty times. I looked up at the white-blue sky, the light purple scars of cloud. Grass clippings stuck to my back and arms. I heard bugs as if they were tunneling in my ears.

I got up, leaned over, waited for my breath, which didn't come. I turned bluish, then green. My brother kicked me softly in the ass, pushed me forward with his heel.

Start the mower. I'm *serious.*

I walked over to the mower. Hot gas fumes blurred the grass ahead of it. Putting my foot on the metal base, I pushed it a few feet forward.

Bill was ecstatic, as happy as I ever saw him, laughing and leaning over and slapping his knee. He flashed his speed-freak tooth-grinding smile.

Practice for the test tonight, he said. Sidekick, stance, frontkick, stance, punch, block, roundhouse.

I saw it coming, saw all that energy coming in slow motion—the tense curve of Michael's ankle, the point of his toe. I didn't even put up my arms. Didn't flinch, duck, or even close my eyes.

Once I was on the ground, everything went still. Things just stopped. I couldn't hear anything. I felt no pain or shame. I was beyond all that, or suffused in it to the extent that it no longer registered as unique. I was a coward, sure, but a hardened one, one who could take a good share of abuse before cracking, which, in my case, usually meant pleading for some kind of amnesty. I thought, for an instant, because I had hit my head so hard on the ground, that I was going to die—that Michael had actually done it this time—right here, alone in my suburban backyard.

Up above me, against a big background of sky, Michael was shirtless, shoeless, wearing only shiny blue Adidas sweatpants with three white stripes down each leg. He crouched, hiking up his pants at the thighs to assure flexibility in the next kick.

Fake the front and roundhouse, said Bill, fake the front and roundhouse.

I got up slowly, not even thinking, not even trying to be defiant, and spit one of those high-viscosity cottonmouth pot lugies right in the middle of my brother's sweaty, muscled chest. Not a cowardly act, and honestly I don't know where it came from.

Michael wiped it off quickly, flung it, stringy, from his fingers. He faked front, roundhoused. I'd seen the move before—was a Bruce Lee fan myself—knew what was coming. I ducked. He missed, landed hard on his back, and immediately jumped up.

Oooh myyy God, said Bill, laughing.

Michael had me on the ground in seconds. He hocked up a good one, spit, and let it hang, thick and lumpy, over my face. I shook my head back and forth, clenched my lips.

Open your fucking mouth, pussy, Bill said. Open it! He's going to spit in your fucking mouth, you motherfucking cock-sucking pussy motherfucker.

You fucker, I screamed, but with my mouth half-closed so he wouldn't spit in it. *Moo fuffer.*

Just as it landed hot and sticky on my face, our neighbor, Mr. Connelly, the guy who had accidentally backed his truck over our dog the year before, came into the yard with a rake.

Leave him alone, he yelled. Michael, let him up. Greg, you want to come over to my house until your mom gets home? Come on. Stay over here for a while, he said, holding the rake, his face red, his giant belly hanging over his belt and jeans.

I wiped my face on my hand, my hand on my jeans. I thought Mr. Connelly was probably glad that I got a good beating. He knew I was a little hellion, mixed up in all kinds of unlawful stuff. I used to grind up his curb with my skateboard. He thought I deserved it, and I probably, for something, did.

My nose bled. Drops of blood spotted the ground in front of me.

No, I managed finally, and I was crying and pissed that I'd let my brother make me cry. I was also pissed at old man Connelly because I hadn't started crying until he'd asked me if I was okay.

I'm fine, I stammered. I'm going inside.

Old man Connelly stood watch, rake in hand, from his yard. Michael started the lawnmower to finish the grass. Bill cruised, blowing me a kiss on his way out of the yard, laughing, rubbing his eyes to mimic crying, flipping me off.

Maybe ten minutes later, as I was looking out the kitchen window after cleaning the blood off my nose and upper lip, tears streaming down my face now that I was alone, I noticed the mower idling by itself in the middle of the yard.

I leaned forward, craned my neck, to see where Michael was, if he was coming inside. What I saw sent a jolt through me. I thought of it later as the most tangible evidence, since the shouting about seeing God four years earlier, of my brother's loosening grasp on the world.

Michael was out by a tree in the corner of the yard. He'd found the sharp stump of a broken-off branch at face level and he was *talking* to it, arguing with the tree or himself, gesticulating as if giving a grand speech, a sermon. He then reared his head back and slammed his forehead onto the branch.

He backed up, blood pouring down his face. I backed away from the window—*what*—went back to the window, thinking my brother was going to kill himself.

He slammed his face on the sharp branch again.

I sat down, dizzy.

Within a few minutes Michael came in the back door, theatrical, absurd. Oh man, he said, blood all down his face. Oh God!

I didn't look up.

Rock flew up and hit me in the head, he said, trying to gauge my expression, my body language. I got what I deserved, you know. I got what I deserved. Right?

I looked at him now, at his forehead. It was a big open gash, fairly serious, a mouth on the wrong part of his face. All the anger seeped out of me. I put ice in a towel and handed it to him. We were standing alone in the kitchen, brothers after school, a slice of twisted Americana.

Blood dripped from the towel onto the kitchen floor, falling in red oblongs, splatting wetly. He needed several stitches, although later he would refuse to go to the hospital, say that he was fine, even though the wound would ooze through the night, making pink circles on his pillows.

He saw the whole thing, he told me. *He* sees everything.

I hoped he meant Bill or Mr. Connelly, but I knew he didn't.

—

His snakes got loose that night. It must have been ten or eleven, maybe midnight. Earlier, just before my father got home, Michael had made a big deal about the incident on the lawn, said he was sorry, that he wasn't really thinking about killing me, acted nicer than he had in months, repeatedly apologizing. Then everyone arrived home—mother, father, my younger brother.

I didn't mention the beating, the bloody nose. After several beatings, this one simply being emblematic, I knew telling was the worst thing, a way of insuring that the next one would be worse. In this way my brother and I became closer in our secrecy, and further from our parents than we already were. My father, if he found out Michael had hit me, would kick Michael out of the house for a few nights and then sulk around feeling bad about it and this, in turn, would make Michael, when he returned, want to kill me all over again, which would make my father kick my brother out, and so on.

Michael and I stuck to the flying-rock story about his wound. I was petrified—of my father kicking Michael out, of Michael coming back and beating me, of Michael killing himself, of the life we were all stuck in. I lived with an almost constant adrenaline flow when I was at home.

We all looked around for the snakes, under beds, behind sofas; in the garage, in tool cabinets, behind an old freezer; my father lifted up heating-duct grates. Nothing.

The next morning I opened up my underwear drawer to three writhing snakes. I jumped back, momentarily panicked.

I called Michael an asshole, told him to take them away. My father, dressed for work, stood in the doorway, not wanting to be bothered by our fighting. All right, you guys, my father said, I'm getting really sick of this.

When my father left, Michael leaned over me, whispered in my ear: It's good to have snakes in your room when you sleep. They absorb your pain while you dream.

I could smell his rotten smoke breath. Get out, I said.

I love you, he said.

Get out.

—

A few weeks after this incident, a neighborhood kid, walking through the woods behind our house, found all three snakes dead. Michael had smashed their heads with a large rock on which he had written the word GOD with a marker pen.

The kid, named Bart, and something of a neighborhood tattletale and nuisance and an avid Eagle Scout, came to our door on a Saturday morning to tell us what he had found, knowing, after seeing Michael in our backyard, that the dead snakes were his.

My mother, still in her bathrobe, with a cup of coffee in her hand, told Bart to go home, that the snakes weren't ours—if there even were snakes out there—and that he didn't know what he was talking about. Bart was thirteen or so and was shocked. He couldn't believe my mother, a soft-spoken, even meek, woman, as generous as anyone I've ever known, the woman who gave the best candy for Halloween, the woman who every kid liked, would *shout* at him. What had gotten in to her? He was just trying to help.

My mother spent the rest of the day trying not to think about the dead snakes and the rock, about what all these clues might be leading to. When I brought up the snakes at dinner that night, one in a gloomy stream of gloomy dinners while Michael was around, my father told me to shut up and eat.

I hate this fucking family, I mumbled.

What?

It's a little late for me to be rambling.

Eat your dinner, smart guy.

JESUS

By the next year, 1986, after burning all of his books on the occult in a fit of satanic paranoia, Michael had begun to study the Bible constantly. It was his way of staving off the demons. A person passing on a street became a message he had to decipher; every face in the window of a school bus was engraved with profound, elusive meaning. He wasn't ill, not in his view, but acutely aware of a deeper world operating inside, or just below, this one.

Time became confused for Michael—it slipped away, sped up, didn't move. Sometimes he'd get stuck inside a minute, get panicky and cry, knowing he might never get out, that time could be solid, tangible; but then he'd blink his eyes and days, weeks, even months had vanished.

He knew that Jesus' forty days in the wilderness were really forty seconds and forty years and forty centuries, too, vision upon vision, each crumbling into the next. What was time for those who believed and would live forever? What was time when life was eternal?

His family existed, for him, in an altered reality, and when we intruded upon his reality, this carefully blown crystal of shifting ideas, there was some degree of violence—always verbal, often physical.

Michael felt he had been sentenced like Jesus, tested while upon this earth by immense cruelties. He was being tested like Job, by the Heavenly Father and he was failing every test. He had evil in him, soul-deep, and he wanted to purge it. He didn't want to hurt people, but he couldn't help it, couldn't control his anger, and the only way to feel any better when he was angry was to hurt someone. And he didn't want his father, his earthly father, to hate him so much. And his brothers—he knew his brothers hated him too. He made his room, blue carpet and rock posters, incense and the purple hue of a black light, a locked temple, as Saint Mark would have called it, a place designed for prayer.

Nights, I would often stand at his door, ear to the wood, and listen to his mumbling, his weeping, his laughing. Downstairs I could hear my mother in the kitchen clanking dishes around, my father on the couch in front of the TV. We never talked about Michael, partly because his insane behavior was "normal" to us, partly because it was too much to deal with to put our feelings into words and exchange them. What was there to say? Or rather, there was everything to say, and with that in front of you language becomes daunting, a burden, a pack of lies and false feelings, a trap you set for yourself, sentence by sentence. My father wanted to watch TV, not talk about Michael. My mother wanted to be busy, doing something, not thinking all the time. I sat around drawing pictures, inventing places not at all like this one.

The year before, Michael had quit school with two months left to go in the year, so in 1986 he was repeating his senior year. And until 1986—despite quitting school, despite all the signs—Michael managed to function without alarming people (other than his family). What I mean is, he was troubled, yes, drug-addicted, sure, violent and depressed, absolutely, but no one could imagine how far this might go, how badly his story might turn out.

The storm was all behind his face, locked down in his skull. He was "crazy," or whatever you want to call it, but he was also very cognizant of others' perception of him. Paranoid schizophrenics, I read years later, sitting in Alderman Library at the University of Virginia while I was a graduate student, are often acutely aware of how others perceive them, delusional as that awareness might be, which makes diagnosis all the more difficult because they are often not honest in describing their thoughts to doctors, whom they may perceive as another cog in the massive conspiracy against them. In other words, schizophrenics are often easily smart enough to tell people what they want to hear. In fact, what we think of as intelligence—the complex processing of information—is only moderately affected by the disease.

Michael saved his strangest behaviors for home. For most of the year he went to school, sat quietly in the backs of classrooms, and went unnoticed in the crowds of students. I noticed him, of course—I thought of him, our life, what the things he did meant, why my family, including myself, seemed to act as if none of this were real—all the time. But in school I tried to pretend that he wasn't my brother, that I didn't even know him.

I attended a high school, like most public high schools, full of troubled kids: heads, loners, future dropouts. It was impossible to tell who would go off, who would go crazy, who would grow out of it. The kid selling dope now could become a corporate lawyer, a missionary, a cop, or a writer within the decade. The one in the chess club, or the Baptist Choir, might waltz in with a shotgun slung over his hip (that same year, a football player at a neighboring high school went to school with his father's .30/30 hunting rifle and shot his girlfriend and himself in the entranceway).

One of my best friends, Sammy, a kid I loved and still have dreams about, was shot in the face and killed at the age of thirteen by a girl whose younger sister he was making out with, or so the story went. (His father, at the wake, squeezed my hand and prayed into my face until I cried and said "please.") The girl who shot him called herself "Purple Haze." She used her father's pistol, which he kept loaded in a drawer by his bed. She was charged with involuntary manslaughter and given probation. Ray, a kid no one talked to, whose girlfriend of four months had recently broken up with him, hanged himself in a tool shed while his father sat in the house twenty feet away watching TV. Lawrence got drunk and flipped his car onto his best friend, Steve, who had been leaning out the window, throwing beer cans, when the car failed to make the turn. I didn't go to the funeral because I had the flu. It was a closed casket and his mother lost her mind and cursed God in front of the minister and the large crowd. By thirteen I was obsessed with death and gloom, the seeming randomness of the world.

My brother, in this context, wasn't as alarming as he might have been. He was odd, depressed, irritable, and volatile, but who wasn't?

—

But then something snapped inside his head. That seems the only way to describe it: a snap, a breaking, a coming undone. He stopped caring about the gaze of others; it was as if he had lost the ability for pretense, and it was as sudden as a gunshot.

In the spring of 1986 he stopped trying to mask his delusions, or he suddenly became incapable of doing so, and now
he didn't try to control himself in public. He'd just turned
twenty and, like my father had done, was struggling to finish
high school. He started carrying his Bible everywhere he
went, one in which he had scribbled notes in every margin.

Ours was a small Southern town—white colonial homes,
churches. Community mattered. Everyone was friendly, even
if only for appearances' sake. My mother and father knew the
principal, the guidance counselor. These people began to feel
sorry for them, concerned, in that administrative way, about
Michael's tenuous—and dwindling—ability to function in
the world. They would call my parents for conferences.
My parents would often cancel, make up some excuse, their
shame over their son having become nearly crippling. My
own embarrassment over my brother's odd religion was at
first debilitating, then simply numbing.

Michael wanted to know the Savior, to memorize the
Word. He would actually use this language—Savior, Word,
Redemption. God was his only chance. Knowing the Bible
was his only way to save himself from what he felt—the anxiety, the voices, the insomnia, his head full of thoughts not
even his.

He became the talk of the town, the bad boy who'd lost
his mind, because of the Bible toting and random quoting of
scripture. He would stop kids on the street, in the school
parking lot, in hallways to remind them of their sins and quote

scripture. He was a kind of village idiot, our small, all-white, suburban school's one truly great spectacle.

Michael's decline, both mentally and physically, was astonishingly fast. He had gone from being a decent student and an amazing athlete to failing everything in the space of four years; had gone from being a black belt in karate—lithe, aggressive, handsome—to being a disheveled, Bible-toting one-man show in less than one year. The rapidity of his decline once he hit twenty—particularly his physical decline—caught us all off guard. His poor marks in school had nothing to do with aptitude, but rather with his shifting of focus. He had a mission in life and little time to pursue other things, even if people insisted these things—school, a job, friends—were important.

His body softened dramatically, his hygiene could produce a gag reflex. Where he had once been inordinately handsome, he now had smears of blackheads across his nose, a double chin, greasy hair. All of this happened so rapidly that when I remember it I think I must be wrong, the physical deterioration must have taken two or three or even five years. But it didn't. It all happened in only several months.

He started smoking three packs of Camels a day, sometimes rocked back and forth uncontrollably in the school smoking section during lunch, looking up through his long bangs at the other dopers to tell them that Jesus loved them, loved us all, that none of us, if we would only believe, would ever, ever die. Eternity was real, he would say, as kids stubbed out their cigarettes and headed inside, laughing. By the end of the year he had the smoking section to himself.

At home he locked himself in his room, smoked, watched evangelical preachers, Robert Tilton mostly, and *The 700 Club* until late in the night, lighting one Camel off another, the sounds of praise, the screams of rapture, brightening his face in blue light, leaking under his door.

His teeth and fingers turned yellow from tobacco tar. He listened to Led Zeppelin, somehow finding a Christian message in it.

He never slept—or if he did, it was maybe an hour or two at a time. He drank huge amounts of Folger's (*only* Folger's) instant coffee from a giant thermos.

Sometimes he'd scream in the middle of the night. None of us dared check on him.

We lived *around* him, not *with* him. He would go days without speaking to any of us. Get home from school, disappear over to Bill's, get high on whatever was available, come home, whispering prayers, talking to himself, the voices and his thoughts his only company. He became the most dogmatically Christian drug addict ever, memorizing—*memorizing*—large parts of both the Old and New Testaments. Everything he said—which was very little—came laced with biblical quotes.

When everyone was in bed, he lurked about the house, hung out in the garage, sitting in a lawn chair, smoking, talking to himself, puzzling over his strange and cruel distance from God.

At two, three in the morning, he cooked, rattled pots and pans. He ate fried bologna, endless cheese slices, bowl after bowl of soggy cereal, instant grits, Wonder Bread, Vienna sausages, beef jerky. He stopped lifting weights and working out. He became as compulsive about eating as he was about smoking or drinking coffee or quoting scripture. My parents told him to go to bed; he told them to fuck off; they went back to bed because they had to get up for work, to start another one of their regimented days. They didn't have time for this. They had busy lives. They couldn't devote all their time to him.

Michael gained thirty pounds in a matter of months. He wouldn't shower unless my father insisted, often with the threat of not giving him any money.

No one knew what was wrong with him. The counselors at school were predictably baffled. He refused to go to psychologists or psychiatrists, and my father subscribed to the shake-it-off, snap-out-of-it, pull-yourself-up-by-the-boot-straps school of manliness, so he wasn't in any rush to take him to doctors, even though he'd watched his own mother temporarily lose her mind years earlier. We all assumed— me, my parents, teachers—that it was another loss, albeit a graphic and uniquely strange loss, to the perils of teen drug abuse.

—

One day the world turned white for Michael. Each object—door, floor, table, human—was wrung dry of all its meaning and he was left floating in a stark nothingness. It was his second severe psychotic break that I witnessed, and it happened during one of the last days of school. He was getting ready to graduate with almost straight Cs and Ds (a gift from his teachers at the insistence of the administration).

It was after lunch, your basic midweek school day—lockers slamming, bits of conversation and gossip drifting through hallways. Michael had just left his remedial math class, where he had realized that the teachings of Jesus were encoded in numbers. He knew His spirit was everywhere, in everything, but he had never considered numbers, never considered looking at the small things, at ideas. It was all bits and pieces, fragments, and no one had told him about the importance of numbers. It was everywhere in the Bible. How could he have missed it? He began to feel a horrible sadness at the fact that he didn't understand math, had never paid attention to it, and now, today, he realized that Jesus Christ, our Savior, our coming Lord, was also contained in numbers and theorems.

Michael floated through the halls in a state of confusion. Faces hovered past like images of faces hovering past, flat and inhuman. The yellow lockers stretched toward the single window at the end of the hall that was now filled with concrete-colored sky.

And then there he was: Jesus Christ, the real guy, the giver of life, the forgiver of sins, the breaker of bread and maker of wine, standing at the end of the hall, suffused in white light, as if in a picture, his hands raised and bloody, a deep wound wet and glistening in his side, a crown of thorns on his head. It was the Christ we've all seen in paintings, except for two modern affectations: a pair of black Levi's 501 jeans and black combat boots.

Michael began speaking in tongues.

Ssshhhaaaaammmmmaaaaaaallaaaaabok.

Kids turned, looked, laughed.

He bumped into the flat, lifeless people—*hey, hey*—walking, then running down the hall.

But then Jesus disappeared, and Michael knew it was because he had failed him, failed Christ, failed God, by being so lazy, by failing to learn what needed to be learned. He looked up at the numbers above doorways. They crushed him with their secrets. They whispered. The numbers were real. If he just concentrated on the numbers he'd be okay, he'd find Christ again; he'd learn about numbers, the curves, the lines, what they meant, how they related to things.

He saw the number 16. It was magical, important, a last tether—he began to cry.

Michael stood in front of room 16, tears streaming hot down his face, dripping off his chin and landing on the floor.

He made squeaking noises; snot bubbled out of his nose; he punched himself in the face, hard, screamed. How could he have missed this?

Kids began to gather around him. Five, ten, fifteen, twenty . . . a crowd.

The hissing was soft, distant. Whispers behind a wall. Snakes behind the glass. Voices in distant regions of his skull. He heard the tears squeeze out of his eyes.

He walked into room 16, sat down among the students, an advanced placement history class. Even though he was crying, he was happy, too, in a way, because now he knew what he had to learn. He started laughing. He was laughing and crying, but he was mostly sad, but then sometimes when he was really sad he couldn't help but laugh at how sad he was. He put his greasy bangs in his mouth and chewed them, sniffling.

Everyone stared silently—at Michael, at each other. He began shaking the desk, tilting it up on two legs.

Miss Smythe, the teacher, was old, popular with students. She walked toward Michael, smiling. Her hair was in the shape of a giant sticky bun, glasses hung off her nose. She wore the bright designer clothes of wealthy Southerners: penny loafers, navy skirts, orange and pink and teal oxford shirts, a scarf.

Michael, she said, but he could barely hear her because she wasn't even real. Michael, this isn't your class, dear. You need to go to your own class now because Jesus Christ died a long time ago and is never coming back; he was just a man, like you. He can't save anyone now. Or maybe you should go to the nurse.

He put his head down, cried harder, began shaking the desk more and laughing; he was a fat, filthy twenty-year-old still in high school, a retard or something, and some of the students had to laugh.

—

The assistant principal, a guy named Kraft with greenish gray hair, came and got me out of my own math class. I started sweating when he said my name. I was sitting in the back of the room, trying to be inconspicuous.

Outside, in the hall, as I stood confused and paranoid, Mr. Kraft explained the problem to me, explained that he wanted me to go get my brother, to try to talk to him, because if anyone came into room 16 he started screaming. He leaned down into my face, his breath nearly toxic—coffee, spearmint, a clogged drain.

All I heard after that was *your brother . . . your brother.* I was in the habit, then, of denying, as much as possible, the existence of my brother, or at least the existence of any relationship between us, or, if that didn't work, I usually pleaded about how ineffectual I was concerning him, how, yeah, he was my brother, but we didn't really communicate much.

I said I couldn't help; I couldn't do it; he wouldn't listen to me. But Mr. Kraft already had me by the arm, leading me to my brother.

We walked down the long halls, past the yellow lockers, past classrooms, past all the kids I knew, the kids I wanted desperately to like me. We walked and walked and I wanted to go home, to walk out the door. My sneakers squeaked, my jeans swished. I could hear the hair move under Kraft's shirt.

The door was open, Miss Smythe standing in the hallway, waiting, I guess, for me, as if I knew what to do.

I sighed, felt faint, but kept walking, listening to my sneakers, my jeans, Kraft's chest hair. I walked into the classroom without looking at anyone, feeling them all looking at me. Why did this have to be *my* brother? What had I ever done?

Someone giggled, but mostly it was all somber silence, the energy having been sucked out of the room. By now some of the kids saw Michael as an actual threat.

My brother had tears streaming down his face, one hanging off his chin. He stopped laughing and crying when he saw me. There we were, staring at each other, in a dead silence except for the low hum of the heating unit, the muffled buzz of the bright fluorescent lights.

I was scared. That's what I remember more than any one detail—that feeling of complete fear and helplessness that would come back to me over the years. Sometimes, even now, almost fifteen years later, when I'm lying in bed with my pregnant wife, in our nice comfortable life, I get this sensation that feels like falling but isn't, and I think, *I once had a brother named Michael,* and this simple fact weighs on me more than my life, weighs more than God, and I spend days afterward depressed, unable to read, unable to work. That day I could taste my fear the way you can taste the beginning of a cold, the way you can taste a penny. This all seemed so much bigger than me. It was so much bigger than me.

I gently touched Michael's arm, unable to think of anything to say. And touching him was a foreign thing, as awkward as a first kiss.

He looked up at me, eyes empty, face shining with tears.

Greg, he said. Jesus. Fuck.

He stood up, simple as that, completely calm. We were face to face. He smelled rotten, as though he hadn't showered in weeks. He smelled of cigarettes, smelled vaguely electric, a smell—almost impossible to describe—that I have come to associate, in recent years, with paranoid schizophrenics. It looked as if he were going to hug me, which he had never done, but he didn't.

Jesus, he said again.

I started walking out of the room and he followed. It was almost the end of the day. I looked back at Kraft and he mouthed the words "thank you."

We walked to the nurse's office, my older brother limping along behind me like a sick child, where he told me an incomprehensible story about numbers and seeing a shirtless Jesus wearing black jeans and boots. We sat there, across from each other, in green, faux-leather chairs, waiting for our mother, who had been called at work. I could see kids drift past the office door, quietly glancing in, whispering to each other.

Michael held his Bible, looked down at his shoes. I stared at him for almost an hour. He sniffled, moved his mouth as if to speak. He had become an alien to me. I didn't know him or understand anything about him. I thought I might cry, but didn't. Not here, not in this closed, incestuous universe of high school, where everyone knew you. I tried to act cool, to find a cool way to sit. I watched the second hand inch around a clock. I waited for our mother.

FLORIDA

That day in school, in room 16 where neither of us should have been, was one of the
last times Michael spoke directly to me, and
it would be years before I tried to understand what he had meant. We never had
much to say to each other, even as children,
but now, once he'd added Jesus to his set list
of hallucinations, he'd lost most of his ability
to speak in any consistently coherent way.

It had been the end of the day, the end
of school, the end, looking back, of any grasp
Michael had on reality. He vanished. He
figuratively vanished that day when he was
twenty. He—figuratively—became a *found-
ling,* a *lost lamb,* a *whore among the city
streets,* a *leper,* a *child of God,* and headed
to "a place in the Hebrew tongue called

Armageddon" (for figurative language there is no better book than Michael's favorite, Revelation). He would never return, never fill out his body again as the person I once briefly knew.

He became a shell full of voices and pain—real, God-drenched pain, the kind of pain that is dangerous to all in its vicinity. You couldn't find him in there no matter how hard you looked. If you caught his eyes, he'd say fuck you. If you walked into a room, he'd walk out, furious. His disease, his spiritual dread, moved to another level.

Every source I've consulted over the years about schizophrenia points to the late teens and early twenties as the most volatile time, the most likely point at which a complete break from reality will occur. I was, after Michael was put away and I'd gotten myself reasonably together, an English graduate student for four years at two different Southern universities, poring over medical texts and psychological journals and religious tracts and apocrypha and transgressive literature in grand, dusty libraries, then writing pedantically complex papers about Dostoyevsky's broken protagonists or Céline's endless rants or Faulkner's wildly dysfunctional Compsons (though I think we were closer to the Snopeses), writing little academic *opera* about the guilt of family, the complex meaning of a single shattered life.

But this is real, not made up, not academic, not figurative: Michael *literally* vanished. It might have been a magic trick, an illusion—the speed with which he was gone. One day, a week after he graduated from high school, just a few weeks after the incident in room 16, his bedroom door—always closed, always locked—was open and he was gone.

A vacant silence filled the upstairs. The air was smoke-colored. I walked into his room, looked around, picking up dirty shirts and socks, kicking over old soda cans, fingering a cheap, silver-plated crucifix on top of a knife-marked mahogany dresser. He had stained the head of Jesus red with magic marker. The smell, again, was that indescribable electric smell that reminds me of mental illness, of halfway houses and psychiatric care and the homeless.

His milky-looking picture of Christ with roving eyes was gone; his scribbled-over Bible, gone. Food cartons, old socks and underwear, dirty tissues, crusty spots on the carpet where he had spit phlegm or shot his seed, half-hung posters, silence. Silence and a giant emptiness. A grand, cavernous emptiness like a tomb, like a church.

My parents, when I asked about him later that night, kept their eyes on dinner and said he'd gone "away," gone "to find a job." There was an air of strange secrecy about the whole thing, a feeling I often got from my parents concerning Michael. I was sixteen now, precocious, inquisitive to the point of annoyance. What did that mean, I wanted to know. Find a job? He was seeing Jesus in school hallways, God in thermal windows, *sacrificing snakes.* What kind of job was he going to get?

He's almost twenty-one years old, my father said, standing in the kitchen after dinner, wearing sweatpants and suede slippers, holding a Diet Coke, the small paunch of his belly pushing out his T-shirt. It's time he took care of himself.

My parents, though very loving while at the same time very busy in that upwardly mobile American way, could not take another day of our life, could not let their home be this dangerous (Mr. Connelly, my rake-wielding rescuer, had come over one Saturday and spoken to my father). And my father had a propensity, a hopefulness, you might say, to believe that a good hard dose of life was always the best medicine. It had worked for him. So Michael, I found out, had been sent away.

—

In the weeks before this, we all hid from each other. We lived in separate rooms. I stayed away from the house as much as possible, hanging out in arcades, at friends' houses. Even Ron and I, who usually at least spoke, grew apart. Part of this was my adolescence, my wish to be free of family; part of it was my secret life of drugs and alcohol; but the biggest reason for it was that we had Michael to think about—our brother, our flesh and blood that we could not understand—every time we were together. Michael was connected to them. I didn't want Michael, so I didn't want them. We were all part of the same problem.

We each lived a private life. We shared space, a roof, nothing else. I've spent many years since that time trying desperately, in different ways, to have an existence exactly the opposite of the one I knew as a boy, and I have largely succeeded, though I still have nostalgic feelings, of course, concerning my mother, younger brother, and father. But any nostalgia, no matter how beautiful or comforting or endearingly sad, eventually leads to Michael and crumbles under the weight of my memory of him.

Just a week before he left, one day after his mostly honorary graduation from high school, which he was asked, politely, not to attend, Michael had made a cross out of baseball bats in our garage, soaked it in lighter fluid, and set it on fire. He had used six Louisville Sluggers that sat languishing in a barrel with footballs and tennis rackets. My father put out the modest blaze with a bucket of water, muttering at Michael, exhausted now, incapable even of yelling.

Smoke had filled the room, however, and alarms went off, the windows went opaque with a yellowish gray residue. Clouds of billowing blue-gray smoke went out into the neighborhood like signals of distress.

A fire truck showed up because Mr. Connelly, our ever-watchful neighbor, had seen the smoke and called. My father, embarrassed, not wanting anyone involved, told them it was an accident—spilled lighter fluid, a match, an honest mistake. They probably would have bought the story until Michael started dancing in a circle in front of them, shouting hallelujah, jigging on one foot to the glory of God, blessing each of them, making a point to touch their jackets and pull his hand away as if they were hot.

My father and the firemen stood in the driveway staring at him, my father beyond speech. The firemen looked at my father, silent, waiting for an explanation, waiting to hear that this was somehow a practical joke. One of the men began laughing and then stopped. My father wouldn't even look at them, instead saying, as he walked off, Thanks. I've got it under control.

My brother no longer had any idea why such a thing was wrong, or dangerous, or antisocial. It had become a part of his thinking, a necessary action to counteract what was happening inside his head at that very moment. He had to set fire to the bats. A black crucifix stayed burned on the concrete for weeks, a reminder.

—

As I have said, my father, like all of us, thought my brother's troubles stemmed from drugs, and partially, of course, they did; this presumed fact made my father completely unforgiving of his behavior. He felt that Michael had brought all of this on himself. He had dropped somewhere between seventy-five and a hundred hits of LSD (a conservative estimate), many of these during the crucial developmental stages of puberty—not to mention all the pot he smoked, the coke he snorted, the mushrooms he ate, the speed he took, and all the rest.

Drugs made Michael's psychosis worse, surely, but they weren't his psychosis. Psychoactive drugs can, obviously, cause harm over extended use, damaging important thought and memory processes. But even the most basic of mental health books will tell you there is no evidence that drug use can cause, or even trigger, the onset of paranoid schizophrenia, though paranoid schizophrenics, once in decline, diagnosed or not, have an extraordinarily high instance of severe drug abuse.

My mother and father, however, weren't the kind of people who went digging through books to look for answers, the way I did long after the fact, long after my brother was locked away. My father, like Michael, had dropped out of high school, only returning at the insistence of my mother when he was almost twenty. My mother and father had grown up on the cusp between lower class and lower middle class, and their parents had no formal education. Drugs were the only thing that made sense for them of Michael's behavior. And who can forgive someone who methodically wrecks his own mind? Who can feel empathy for a person, son or not, like that?

—

My mother and father, I eventually learned, had given Michael five hundred dollars in cash and a one-way ticket to Orlando, Florida. We all needed him out of our everyday lives—we were all exhausted, on edge. And he was skirting the edge of some huge tragedy. We could all feel it coming. I could feel it. The probability of his doing something irrevocable kept me up at night. I thought he might kill himself and I'd have to find the body. I thought he might want to kill me, as he had threatened, or, worse, my mother, whom he had begun to hover around like a fly, always keeping his eyes on her no matter where she went in a room. I'd feel the blood rush in my temples when he got near the kitchen knives, or had a lighter in his hand, menacingly flicking it.

My parents chose Orlando because they had read that, aside from Las Vegas, it was the city with the most job vacancies (the flash and brightness and noise of Las Vegas would probably send a schizophrenic hiding in the sewers; although the animal mascots of Disney World couldn't be much better).

My mother had spent days on the phone contacting the employment office of Disney, trying to get Michael a job as a janitor, a food vendor, anything, still believing he could somehow hold down work. She set up several interviews for him. This sounds absurd in hindsight, but my mother still had hope, was always willing to try. She made it so all he had to do was walk into the right office and remain calm and he'd have a low-wage, low-interaction job. They also offered low-rent housing for park employees.

My father thought someone might just pull him off the street to work—labor, construction, lawn care. He might straighten out once he saw that he had to. He might check himself into a hospital. One thing was for sure, though, he could not live at home. He could live on the street. He could go to jail. He could even die. But my father was not letting that drug-addicted loser back into this house he was still try-ing to pay for.

—

My life improved. I could not have missed my brother less. I'd wake up every morning happy that he was gone. My family would eat breakfast together, which we hadn't done in years, and it was as if he had been erased. I can't even explain what it was like to be free of him. It was like finding out you didn't have cancer anymore, I imagine, or that your newborn baby was healthy after all, that it was just a smear on the X-ray of its chest. A wave of such overwhelming relief fell about our house that I remember at one point simply breaking down in tears, actual tears of happiness, when I picked up a butcher knife and it didn't seem like anything but something you used to cut chicken or celery.

In fact, his absence from our lives was such a relief that it was only then that I realized the true extent of the turmoil he, or his disease, had caused. My family took a vacation to Nags Head, North Carolina, and we laughed and went out and ate seafood and no one stared at us—a real family vacation. Dur-ing the day, I surfed while Ron made sand castles and my par-ents lay on the beach holding hands, like newlyweds.

This kind of happiness was bizarre, alien. We were so starved for it that all we wanted was life without small tragedies, without violence and anger and uncomfortable silence. Heaven, for us, was not expecting a call at four in the morning. Heaven was not having to sleep with your bedroom door locked.

—

Six months passed, six eventless months. Ah, the beauty of inertia, the grace of absolute, mind-numbing suburban ennui.

I stopped thinking of Michael because I blissfully had no knowledge of the future, no inkling of the shape of this story.

My parents had their friends over to the house without the possibility of something surreal happening—a fire, or a sermon on the Sodomites. They had parties. I had girlfriends over. My younger brother had friends sleep over and watch movies and play video games. So this was life, we thought. Not bad.

Michael did, however, call home several times from Florida, crying, but my parents kept me in the dark about his whereabouts and well-being. I didn't care; I didn't ask. I'd ask my mother who had called and she'd hesitate and say, No one, your aunt, no one.

My mother worried privately, and sent Michael cash overnight several times. My father took a sterner stance— Michael was an adult who had proven himself to be worthless, criminal; they had given him money and a chance and that was enough.

—

It didn't last. Six months after he left, almost to the day, Michael showed up at the door—just like that, no warning, nothing. A knock at the door and there he was.

He stood in the doorway, suffused in sunlight, near death. He had lost forty pounds, had almost starved. He stared, wide-eyed, eyes sunk deep in their sockets, and at first I don't think he recognized anyone but my mother. He didn't know what day or month it was, didn't know his middle name, couldn't remember what state he had just been in, when or where he was born.

He said, I think I'm very old and hungry. I went to school. I was born in a manger. I am very old and hungry.

Pale, sick, mouth agape, bewildered to the point almost of catatonia, sitting on the couch as skinny as a concentration camp prisoner from a scratchy Nazi-era documentary, he looked like someone else entirely. I couldn't believe it was him. We all stood around in the living room as if we'd just seen a spaceship land, as if we were characters in a cruel art film and we didn't know our lines.

I couldn't not look at him, though I tried. He smelled like trash, stared straight ahead, his head leaning back on a cushion, staining it with grease. His hair was long; he had a thick beard. His eyes were glassy and distant. The fly on his tattered, dirt-stained jeans was open, his shoes were untied and almost black with filth. He was helpless. It was the saddest thing I have ever witnessed. I wanted to scream, but couldn't. I lost something of myself that day, and I've never gotten it back. Standing in the room with him, needing to scream, to shout, to break something, but unable to, I said to myself, I'm going to go crazy; I'm going to be like him; I feel it coming.

My father broke down completely, sobbing, hugging Michael, and then sitting down and laying his head on the kitchen table—my stoic father, my tough, no-bullshit father destroyed by a guilt you could almost see around him like a luminous aura.

Michael didn't move, didn't even eat, until my parents took him to the emergency room, simply not knowing what else to do. The nurses gave him fluids and a meal. They checked his blood for drugs and alcohol, but there was no trace of either.

—

Years later, when my brother was in prison, I heard the stories about Florida from my younger brother, whom Michael had confided in one day.

Michael was kicked out of a youth hostel the first day he arrived, then had lived in a small Assembly of God church for the first few weeks. The pastor let him sleep there on a cot, but wouldn't let him attend church. Michael was too disturbed, too likely to have outbursts of religious zeal that scared people, even charismatics and evangelicals, who were having outbursts of their own for the Lord. At the best of times, while Michael was living at home, his appearance was frightening; away from the constant care of my mother, the sight of him was enough to make people cross the street. He looked, at his worst, unmedicated—unshaven, yellow teeth, hair everywhere—something like Linda Blair in *The Exorcist*. His looks, and his vastly unstable behavior, were exactly what got people burned at the stake in medieval times, or had their skulls drilled open so the spirits could escape, or had leeches placed on their eyelids to drain the evil energy from inside their heads. Florida wasn't so much better than this.

Other details of his journey are murky, not grounded by any specific narrative, time, place.

He was gang-raped while living among the homeless.

He paid for hookers, both male and female, with money he stole from other homeless kids; he once beat a hooker (a woman, I think) nearly to death in an abandoned house because she tried to steal his Bible, then went to a convenience store and called an ambulance.

A trucker gave him money and food, in exchange for blow jobs until Michael finally tired of him and moved to a different part of town, found a different group of kids, a different corner to hang out on.

He was robbed.

He participated in, or at the very least was present during, both rapes and robberies.

He prostituted himself for money or coffee or food or drugs.

He prayed several times a day.

A demon lived in his shoes, so he threw them away and stole a pair off a sleeping drunk.

He became seriously ill after snorting crank and was taken to an emergency room, where he was treated for extreme dehydration and cramps. He had no identification, no money. His wallet had been stolen and the only thing he had was his tattered Bible that had his name written in the front.

When the hospital called my mother, having somehow tracked her down about the bill, Michael had already vanished. My mother wanted to go to Florida to look for him, but my father vetoed this, and said that they'd never find him anyway.

Michael also had begun to hallucinate almost constantly. He saw and heard demons in malls and car washes and restaurants. He began to believe my father was sending them. He no longer felt strong surges of schizoid paranoia, evil smoldering at the periphery; he *was* paranoia, and reality, our reality, was now at the far periphery.

His confusion made him cry, strike out at people, create huge scenes in convenience stores, shopping centers, on street corners, spewing epithets with the words "thou" and "thee" all mixed up with potty talk and quotations from Revelation.

He was arrested at least twice for shoplifting and being drunk in public, though he wasn't drunk. He must have thought that Florida was hell, a place to torture and be tortured, a place where God forgot about you, where everything that could go wrong went wrong. It had literally drained the life out of him.

When he returned to us from the hospital after overnight observation, he began his visits to psychologists, psychiatrists, counselors, and rehab. He was almost twenty-two, and in many ways this was only the beginning.

SCIENCE

I have never felt more guilt than I did on the day I found out my brother was an acute paranoid schizophrenic, when I found out, finally, what all of this was. It was the opposite of the relief and elation I felt over his absence, my freedom from him. Fear is transient. Guilt, believe me, lingers.

I was seventeen, a freshman at a local state university, which was forty minutes from my parents' home. It suddenly, somewhat inexplicably, felt like my fault, all of it: his whole life, our whole lives. I started replaying everything I'd ever said about him, all the cruelest words: when I'd told everyone in school about his masturbating and they'd called him "beater"; or the time I'd told one of his old friends about the night after the Ozzy Osbourne concert, the seeing God, calling my brother "Angelhead," some conflation of pothead and lunatic—and the boy, one of Michael's only remaining friends, never called him again; and there were so many more instances, piling up as evidence against me, pointing to how despicable, thoughtless, and heartless I had been toward my own brother.

I still feel it sometimes, the guilt. I don't mean I remember how it felt, or that I can approximate the feeling again by fixing on a certain memory that seems to evoke it; I mean I can still, to this day, feel the guilt, *the same exact guilt* I felt that day, as if it is somehow stored up in me, a part of who I am.

My mother told me of the diagnosis while sitting at our kitchen table. All the doctors had been saying he was chronically depressed, strung out. He had a personality disorder, maybe brain damage from some environmental cause, a shoddy birthing procedure. He needed more guidance. He needed moral support. He needed love. He needed lithium. He needed Prozac or Zoloft. He needed direction. He needed to get clean. A Catholic doctor asked my parents if they had thought of taking him to church.

Finally a doctor named Smith, a psychiatrist, put Michael through weeks of tests. He came back with a diagnosis of acute paranoid schizophrenia the day after the results came in. He couldn't believe no one had thought of this. Michael did not have a split personality or mental retardation or manic-depressive psychosis; he didn't have a borderline personality or a brief psychotic disorder or street-drug psychosis or prescription-drug psychosis; he didn't have psychosis because of other diseases, such as a brain tumor or viral encephalitis or temporal-lobe epilepsy or cerebral syphilis or Huntington's disease or AIDS or other AIDS-related symptoms; he didn't have narcolepsy or progressive supranuclear palsy or metachromatic leukodystrophy or congenital calcification of basal ganglia, although some doctors might point to one or some of these.

No, Michael was a textbook case, right down to the delusions and physical deterioration coming on in his late teens and early twenties. Michael, said Dr. Smith, had been essentially creating an alternate reality over the years by mixing up myriad aspects of actual reality into something no one but he could truly understand. That's what made the disease so damaging and hard to treat. You couldn't address the problem—the mix-up in the brain, my brother's thoughts—you could only medicate and regulate the outward symptoms (psychotherapy wouldn't work in a case as severe as Michael's). You couldn't unravel the delusions and get him on track again, you could simply make it so the brain functioned at such a stunted level that the delusions ceased or were broken up into incomprehensible fragments of thought and, with luck, into "normal" thought patterns.

The doctor said that 400,000 homeless people were afflicted with the disease; that almost two million people had the disease in the United States, about as many as live in

Miami or San Francisco. Imagine that, a whole city of schizophrenics among us. This didn't help.

I have an image of my mother staring at the dark wood of our kitchen table, saying, I don't know what we're going to do, saying this with no inflection, like the undead talking in a late-night movie. It was February. There was cold, sharp light in the room. A pitiful midday sun made geometric shapes the color of stained teeth on the kitchen floor. My mother, after hearing the news, barely spoke for days. My father sat in his favorite chair, the TV droning on in front of him, but he wasn't even looking at the screen; he seemed to be looking at the blank wall behind it.

It seemed so obvious once I knew—not that he was schizophrenic but that he was definitely severely mentally ill. I had known many "burnouts" or "heads" at school of one degree or another—I was, in a way, one myself—but no one came close to my brother's strangeness. Now I knew he was ill, but I had no understanding of paranoid schizophrenia that day—its massive delusions, the hallucinations, the blending of color and sound, the accumulation of facts—memories, television, history, religion, books, all manner of cultural and personal artifacts—and how they came together to form completely new and alternative notions of self and reality.

Some schizophrenics, with the right psychotropic drugs, manage to function "normally." Because of its early onset, however, my brother's case was so severe as to be nearly hopeless—possibly contained but never genuinely improved without huge advances in the study and treatment of the disease.

It would be years later, after reading an endless stream of books about both religion and madness, before I felt I had any understanding, and then only some, because the mind of another is ultimately unknowable; you can only approximate it with metaphor, invention, language, story; you can only impose meaning after the fact.

I knew he was sick. And, most important, I realized for the first time it wasn't his fault. I had blamed Michael, hated Michael, for his behavior. So finding out suddenly, nearly a decade after his first psychotic break, that none of the behavior was entirely his fault, was nearly unbearable, making us all—particularly my father and I—feel immoral and ruthless to such a degree that shame is not a strong enough word.

My brother spent the next several months going through tests, taking different medications, derivatives of the major tranquilizer phenothiazine, to quell some of his more severe delusions. Standing in a cold, white room with generic prints on the wall, Dr. Smith, a long-nosed, balding man in khakis, tennis shoes, and a denim shirt, the kind of man you can't imagine as anything but a doctor, told my parents that often delusions were of a religious nature. In evaluating these visions or delusions, it is important, he said, to realize they are culture-bound. Many schizophrenics talk to or hear or see "God"; some think they are vampires; others believe the CIA and the president are out to get them; many believe their thoughts are being broadcast over television or radio.

He mentioned books, support groups. He was well-meaning but cold. He smiled, but acted as if he didn't want to be more involved than necessary. He knew how these things went—every day he saw what the disease did to young people and their families. It could be dangerous if the delusions continued unchecked, because they tended to get more elaborate, more undeniably the patient's *actual* reality. Michael showed extreme violent tendencies. Schizophrenics as a populace have a much higher instance of committing both murder and suicide (just during the writing of this book I have tallied six national news stories about paranoid schizophrenics committing homicide or multiple homicide, and those, mind you, are only the ones making the *national* news, like the Unabomber). Violence against family is most common.

If we lived in an Islamic country and the available cultural symbols and metaphors were Allah and Muhammad, Dr. Smith told my parents, he'd see and hear them; the same would be true in a country where the prevailing belief was Hindu, or Buddhist. It was a way of dealing with severe emotional pain, depression. Externalized by the sufferer, it was the devil, a huge political conspiracy, whatever. Intense internal (emotional) conflict needs signifiers. The hope for a cure, the cure itself, has a name, too: God. Good and Evil. Hope and Despair. The rigid standbys of cultural meaning.

Michael was using the available terms to name his nightmares. They were real to him, of course, but they came from within. There was still a lot about schizophrenia to learn, Dr. Smith continued. Studying the mind, all the ways it can go wrong, is like studying outer space: endless.

He looked at his watch, wished them luck. He smiled. Here were a few pamphlets.

My parents felt stranded in a new wilderness without a map. My mother kept thinking: Murder? Suicide?

Specialists analyzed my brother's thoughts via basic question and answer, measured the chemicals in his brain, the deterioration of his body. (Acute paranoid schizophrenics rarely live to an advanced age because of physical deterioration brought on by diet, lethargy, and poor hygiene.) We learned that 25 percent of schizophrenics recovered (generally mild, late-onset cases), but 15 percent killed themselves and another 25 percent had to be hospitalized and under constant supervision. There were theories that posited the disease resulted from defects in the limbic system, others that cited genetics, others still that said it was environmentally and culturally bound, a by-product of living in a polluted mental environment, the modern world. It was like learning a new language.

Michael was back living at home now. We all felt suddenly caring because of our guilt.

He spent most his time, those first weeks, sitting in a chair on the opposite side of the room from my father's chair in our den. One day he was watching Robert Tilton speak in tongues on the large TV that organized the room. I stood in the doorway. I've read that many schizophrenics don't like TV; it jumbles their thoughts. But Michael loved TV. It was up there with cigarettes and coffee and marijuana. He believed Robert Tilton was a medium, delivering messages from God directly to him; any money he had went either to marijuana purchases, his favorite thing, or to the Robert Tilton Ministries in Dallas, Texas: two, three, five crumpled dollars in an envelope with a barely legible address and "God Bless Us All" for a return address.

He got up and touched the television screen. He was wearing jeans and an old flannel shirt that lifted up as he bent over, revealing the tops of his buttocks. He had gained most of his weight back over the last few months with compulsive eating. A black woman was being healed of cancer on the screen. Tilton spoke in tongues: *Oooosssssaaaaalllaaaamaaaayaaa-ooobajjaaaa.*

I leaned against the doorframe, my arms crossed so he understood I didn't mean to be aggressive. I asked him, as politely as possible, just above a whisper, what Tilton was saying.

Michael didn't answer. He wasn't finished listening to God.

I waited. My mother was doing dishes in the kitchen behind me. When insanity is routine, you learn to function around it, you learn that the dishes still have to be done and the lawn needs cutting, you have to go to work and school and have Christmas and birthdays and pay the bills.

During a commercial, I asked again.

He looked at me, almost smiling. I asked again.

He told me that he was asking God to take him. He said that they were trying to trick him and that he didn't know who to believe anymore.

What do you mean, trick you? Who's trying to trick you? The doctors?

Them, he said, scanning the room with his eyes, as if pointing them out to me.

Them?

He walked out of the room, bumping me as he passed, as if I wasn't even there.

———

Doctors told my parents different, divergent stories that intersected at points but never made a coherent narrative. Some thought it was all chemical, all biological, curable through science and medicine. They showed pictures of a schizophrenic's brain with enlarged cerebral ventricles like glowing butterflies. Others thought it was cultural, environmental. The number of schizophrenia cases diagnosed has risen sharply, in direct correlation, some say, to the rise of a frenetic, overwhelming popular culture and endless cultural stimuli and, of course, a fragmenting of anything like concrete meaning (though the increase in numbers of cases could also quite simply be a part of the higher numbers of diagnoses of all mental ailments). According to this environmental argument, which is generally frowned upon by the leaders in the field, schizophrenia might be considered a postmodern disease. (Interestingly, there are almost no reported cases among the rural Amish; largely isolated American Indians on reservations have had a remarkably low instance of the disease also.)

Statistics and more statistics. Almost 8 percent of inmates in prisons are possibly schizophrenic. Schizophrenics are 500 percent more likely to kill themselves than the general population. Only about 60 percent of schizophrenics receive treatment. Almost a quarter of schizophrenics could live independently at some point after being treated, but these are generally the mild cases. Learn from the numbers. Tally your chances. This many humans had this happen to them. This many had that. Do you see any answers in these graphs?

What was agreed upon was that whatever the origins of Michael's schizophrenia, it was serious, "chronic," and "acute"—to the point that he would never believe he was ill, but rather that the doctors and my parents were yet more players in the conspiracy against him. He could only trust God. There was hope, but only some. New medications came on the market all the time—Clozaril, Loxitane, Orap, Haldol, Compazine, Prolixin, Stelazine, Mellaril, and many others.

These might work. Things could change. But don't hold your breath.

It was probably hereditary, said Dr. Smith, but maybe not. It was treatable with medication, but only to a point, and only in some cases. *His* case is severe, so don't be too hopeful. Yet don't give up hope.

When you read about schizophrenia, you can begin to believe it is disembodied, abstract, simply *out there,* not actually having to do with human beings, with teenagers and young adults, with families. I stare at homeless people, wondering. I listen closely to stories about people who can't function at home or school. The stories that interest me are the ones about those on the fringes of society. I scan the paper for stories of people dying on the streets, winos beaten to death by kids, old men stepping in front of trains. I think, Why?

Do you have a history of mental illness in your family? they asked my parents.

My mother's family, no. My father's family tree, as I said at the beginning, was twisted and gnarled with alcoholism, depression, suicide.

He said not that he knew of.

We'll do what we can, said the doctors, but it will be hard, at times harder than you might imagine. However, knowing exactly what was wrong with him was a step in the right direction. Drug abuse made things worse, but this, his illness, was probably inevitable, perhaps encoded in his DNA at birth, though don't blame yourselves. The message: It's not your fault; there's not much you can do; the best thing is heavy tranquilizing medications, psychotropics. Try to get him someplace where they can deal with him safely. Here are some hotlines, the number of a good social worker, some prescriptions. Get yourself in a group, get help. You can't put him in a hospital, I'm afraid; that's a violation of his rights. Call me if it's an emergency. I don't work Saturdays.

The diagnosis helped, but it also made my parents angry, untrusting; they had been told by several psychologists and counselors over the years that Michael was depressed and needed to stop taking drugs. Both true, but only part of the story. They thought they had sent their troubled, violent, moody, drug-addicted son to Florida to get a job and straighten up. They had sent a sick kid—criminal or not—to slaughter. They never got over that.

DELINQUENTS

After the diagnosis came rituals as regular as clockwork, mixtures of old-time religion and television and slapstick: my brother putting a lawn chair in the middle of the yard, dancing around it, filthy and bloated, falling down, praying for God to take him away, strike him down, finish him off. Our neighbors stood on their porches wondering whether to call the cops or an ambulance; neighbors scratching their heads then, I imagined, relaying stories of my brother, their bizarre neighbor, over phone lines across neighborhoods, cities, counties, states, a continent.

Our family dog, a docile mutt named Molly, wouldn't go near Michael because of something he'd done to her, some kick across the yard because she housed demons, or maybe he thought he'd kill her one day to save her from the world, and she sensed the menace in the same way dogs sense fear.

Crosses appeared in odd places, formed from the stuff of suburban existence—place mats, welcome mats, rugs, gardening tools, sporting equipment; anything could be made into a crucifix, our barbecue a makeshift altar. Money disappeared. It all went to snack cakes and Fritos and bags of cheap pot, and to Robert Tilton, that shyster to the poor—bills crumpled and scribbled on, *God bless you, God bless us.* He'd get back a Gideon, a generic thank-you note, and a bookmark that Tilton's tears had supposedly dried on.

My parents couldn't take any more. They became much closer during this time, hunkered down, devising plans of dealing with Michael late at night. They were a team in crisis. They weren't so much a couple as two people pitted against an unconquerable foe, stuck with their family and their lives. Even if Michael was sick, they couldn't live like this. Even if there was lingering guilt over sending him to Florida, where he nearly died, where horrible things happened to him, this was unbearable. God and the devil, what Dr. Smith would call *the apotheosis of mental anguish,* were becoming less and less abstract—not just to Michael, but now to us.

My mother had moments when she believed he had become simply and purely evil, beyond all help. When she was around him her hands would shake involuntarily. Yet she never stopped loving him, or at least the memory of who he had been, long ago, as a boy, even when Michael would stand in the kitchen behind her, puffed up and slightly shaking, as if just barely containing his rage. She had dreams of him red-eyed and snarling. She wanted to find a way to help him, but how long could she live like this—sneaking around the house, locking doors, peeking around corners, listening for footsteps. This is a haunted house, she thought. We live in a haunted house.

—

I stayed in my college apartment in Norfolk, though I only sporadically attended classes. I had trouble seeing the point of college. My classes early on seemed ludicrous in their insistence on rote memorization, in their use of Scantron sheets where you simply chose the correctly memorized answer that coincided with A, B, C, or D.

My parents thought of college as more of an idea than something real, something tangible and day-to-day, because no one in my family had ever gone to a university. My father had been the second in his family to finish high school. My parents paid for my apartment, financially stretching themselves even thinner, just to keep me away from Michael, to afford me a "normal college experience."

I had roommates at first—I'd always been adept at hiding my problems, offering a smile when appropriate, looking healthy and fine, always quick with a joke—but as my brother's condition declined, I withdrew from the world, needing to live alone, to sit around and read all the books I'd suddenly discovered and obsess about my family, my brother.

My method at college was to sign up for several courses, then figure out which ones would be the most enjoyable and require the least effort; I'd attend those courses and drop the rest, in an effort, I told myself, to work on my writing, to have time to think and read, because now I was going to be a writer, even if that meant poverty and obscurity. I needed to make sense of my world, needed to try to understand people below the surface, the artifice, of life.

At some point—I can't pinpoint exactly when—I realized that books made sense of the worst things, even if they seemed stunted and dark, offering nothing but a crippled epiphany. These were the ones I gravitated toward then: Poe, Dostoyevsky—"The Tell-tale Heart" and "White Nights" are, to me, schizophrenic classics—and the American pulp novelists of midcentury. I began reading all the time, endlessly, book after book, always looking to find the grand tragedy rendered with meaning—the more transgressive, the more violent, the better, because by the middle of the book I wanted to see how this mess would be fixed, how a life, even a sad, broken, imaginary life, could be *saved*. I started to believe—and I still believe—that I could somehow save myself with a story, and even though I couldn't save anyone else, I could try to understand them, attempt to grant them at least that, and perhaps it is in this, this attempt to understand, that a person is truly saved.

I'd skip weeks of classes but read all the books for a course and be led, by those books, on to other books. After reading a bent, rumpled copy of *Zen and the Art of Motorcycle Maintenance* by Robert Pirsig, that quintessential and half-baked text of the hippie ethos, I decided grades didn't matter, organized education was a farce, and all true learning was heuristic (this is the effect a burgeoning intellectual life had on me: I began to view everything as suspect, if not outright false, which took me back to my punk childhood).

This new attitude—laziness disguised as rebelliousness—freed up a lot of time. My *sitting around and thinking* was now justified in big words and Eastern ideas filtered through the counterculture and pop psychology and philosophy.

Reading was what I loved, still love, true, but at the same time, looking back, I was afraid that if I didn't make my mind strong, I'd lose it, just like Michael had. I was afraid that wave of insanity, the currents of which I knew were already in my blood—I thought I could feel them like an itch at the base of my skull sometimes at night—would close over me if I didn't prepare myself, if I didn't constantly read and spend all my time building up my defenses against unreasonable thoughts, if I didn't engage all troubling ideas, cut them off at the pass, and bend them into tolerable, understandable things.

I found Calvino and Bruno Schulz and Beckett and Borges while sitting around, hanging out in libraries, skipping classes—all writers, in my mind, compelled to map the devolution and fissures of the mind in extraordinary ways. I went on, later, to get three rather impractical English degrees, my way of buying time to learn how to learn and to write, and still think of my education—or the part of my learning that actually matters—as something I figured out on my own, though I realize this is a romantic and mostly false notion, probably something I first came across in that Pirsig book.

Michael had drowned in thoughts and ideas, twisted notions of the metaphysical. More than anything, I did not want to be my brother. I did not want to suffer as part of my family; I wanted, foremost, somehow to be free of connection to these people, whom I desperately loved; barring that, I wanted to be *philosophical* about them and our lives. I am not exaggerating when I say books saved my life; or, put another way, books saved my mind and helped me to learn how to understand my life.

—

Michael told my parents, in one of his moments of psychotropic lucidity, that he had met two friends at the mall. He wanted to move out, to move in with them. He hated my parents now, he decided, wished them dead. Sorry, I love you, he said.

My mother often dropped Michael off at the mall like a teenager, the only way she could get him out of the house now that even Bill, the speed freak, the collector of porn and continuous enrollee in junior-college business courses, had abandoned him. Mall security guards had called my parents several times. They'd call to say that Michael stalked women, made lewd gestures to kids, told a woman he wanted to baptize her baby.

My mother took him back, again and again. That's where he wanted to be, smoking on a bench in the mall, staring at all those people with their secrets. And what else was there to do? She couldn't find anywhere else to put him.

Dealing with insanity became about improvisation and compromise, figuring out minor solutions while looking for a big solution. The hospitals she'd contacted about Michael were taking months to get back to her. Her job became putting out emotional fires around the house. Michael would get angry—she'd distract him with a promised trip to the mall. He'd start chanting and rocking—she'd ask if he wanted to go to McDonald's for a shake or a sundae; he'd look up and smile like a five-year-old. Bargaining became her way of dealing.

Frazzled, depressed, stressed beyond what is tolerable by Michael's presence at home, she told him he could move in with the "two friends."

He was an adult. Wasn't he?

My mother and father were relieved and didn't think to meet the two men with whom Michael was moving in. They were two guys who had an extra room, nothing more. And what if my parents found out the two men were dangerous, mentally handicapped ex-cons or totally imaginary? Michael would have to keep living at home. And any questions would have brought on a violent tantrum, anyway. In many ways my brother was like a child you could never discipline.

They figured as long as he took his medication every day he could function. The one constant about my family was our ability to downplay all the negative possibilities, to pretend, to go from small trauma to small trauma, somehow hoping that tomorrow, or the day after, things would start to get better.

At about this time, my parents' request to put him on social security for a disability came through. He could pay the rent himself. They weren't kicking him out, not like before; he *wanted* to go, to get out into the world, to try to live a normal life. Even Dr. Smith agreed it could be a good thing for him.

—

He had met the men in the food court of the mall. They were white, college-aged, but they didn't go to college. They worked construction, commuted to Yorktown every day to work on a new naval weapons station as laborers. They hung out at the mall on Saturday afternoons, ate pizza at the Sbarro, caught a movie if anything good was playing; if not, they hit the game room, dropped quarters in machines, leaned and cursed at the blinking lights and noise of a race car game.

The two men had a history together. They were real people, which is sad, because I don't want real people like them to exist. But they do. Their story went something like this: They had met as boys in a juvenile institution where they had both been sent for burglary. They became friends because of a common interest in pool, women, movies, dope. They wore track suits and expensive basketball shoes; one had a pocket watch, the other long brown hair. They smoked cigarettes. That's all I really know about them.

They met Michael as he rocked back and forth on a bench in the food court, one of the several retarded or homeless people who spent afternoons at the mall. The real specifics of the meeting, what was said, the body language, the subtle gestures, the way people, even delinquents, interact nervously on first meetings are unimportant.

Michael was smoking a cigarette like a prisoner on death row, as if it were his last, always his last, inhaling with exaggerated need. The skin between his fingers was yellow. The voices chattered endlessly. He prayed once an hour, when the long hand hit the six on the clock near the theater. He wasn't sure God cared about him anymore. He had a brown circle on his front teeth the exact size of the end of a cigarette filter.

Maybe they made fun of him at first, but Michael didn't understand, didn't get it, his ability to decipher humor long gone, which made fucking with him even funnier to the two men.

They talked. Maybe they laughed. Certainly dope was mentioned. And they all stood up and walked away, as simple as that, two criminals on probation, with my brother in tow like a kidnapped kid. They lived near the mall.

At their place, they smoked good dope, indica, thaistick, sinsemilla. They used a glass bong with a skull sticker on it.

They turned on Public Enemy, the bass beat, the sampled screech. They ate popcorn, watched Hitchcock's *The Birds* on TBS and the first half of *Under Siege* on video. They slow-motioned violence, chugged beers in some kind of drinking game Michael didn't quite get—having to do with the crunch of bones and punches thrown. Chug, they'd yell, and Michael would chug. He was like a pet, a toy. He laughed like a true moron.

On the day he moved in with the two men, my mother packed him bags of clothes, towels, sheets, as if for a child going to camp.

She dropped him off, told him to call home later, told him to have fun and be polite. My brother, bearded, overweight, nearly galloped up the stairs to his new apartment on the second floor of a complex that had a faux-Tudor feel to it and nice landscaping, too.

The first few nights went well. Or at least there were no phone calls home. Dope, movies, snacks. Laughter, music, pushing and clowning around, jumping up and down when the music and drugs called for it, banging on the floor when the downstairs neighbors banged on their ceiling, laughing because, fuck them, fuck those neighbors, man, motherfucking welfare-gettin' losers. Whatever the two guys thought was funny, Michael laughed at. He still heard voices, even warnings, but they were underneath this bubble of happiness and connection. It had been years since he'd had a friend, much less two.

—

But at the end of the first week he called my mother. He was alone in the apartment. He begged her to come get him, but not to bring my father. The guys he was living with were working, getting overtime on a Saturday at the weapons station. She asked if he had taken his medicine. He said yes.

Sensing a real problem, my mother agreed and drove the ten miles to get him. He had sounded urgent, but it was hard to tell what that meant with Michael. He reacted to dreams and imagined things as if they were real. Robert Tilton speaking in tongues on TV might send him into a funk as deep as if someone he loved had died. And the real stuff, the stuff that ought to upset a person, he often missed. She tried not to think about it. She couldn't bring up anything else to think about. An image of her son replaced the highway and strip malls. She wondered how life had become like this. She knew, of course, knew the facts, but she couldn't trace things back and make much sense. She had been beautiful, a popular girl in school, with friends and dreams. She fell in love with my father, who was maybe a little gruff, maybe he had a bad temper at times, but his heart, she knew, was good, and when he was in a good mood, he was funny and laughed a lot. She loved his smile, his face, those sad eyes. He was passionate, she thought, and for any anger he showed there was more than an equal and opposite reaction of love, more passion, a complete, even suffocating, devotion to the things he cared for most. There were babies, picnics, relatives, school pictures, sports . . . time slipped, sped ahead . . . but at some point, and she couldn't even remember when now because it was so long ago, Michael had changed, had gotten darker and stranger and unknowable, and everything had begun to crumble and rot. And then here she was, driving to get him.

It was a perfect spring day. The Virginia sky, in the spring when the humidity is low, is vibrant and crayon-blue, and now it filled up her windshield. She listened to the oldies station, the Ronettes, the Beach Boys, nostalgic for her youth, being in her twenties, feeling love the way you do when you're young.

Michael was an emotional mess, she thought, untrustworthy. Probably nothing had happened and he just missed the comforts of home, where she bought any food he wanted, gave him his medication on time, drove him to the mall, to the doctor, let him watch religious television all day as he rocked and smoked, sometimes calling her a cunt, a bitch, as she brought him cheese and crackers, bowls of soup. It was like she had to keep a lid on a boiling pot.

Pulling into the parking lot, she saw him sitting on the curb with his head between his knees. She couldn't believe how heavy he'd become, how the antipsychotics and antidepressants and sleeping pills, those endless bottles of expensive pills that still barely contained him, had made it even worse.

She almost started crying. My mother has an astounding ability to ignore the harshest realities, to hover above even death and depression and mayhem and float through the day, somehow, smiling. I deplore and admire this ability by turns. But today, looking at him touched something raw in her mind. All the stuff inside her started coming to the surface. He looked like a bum, a wino, and he was still just a boy in her eyes. Despite everything, she still loved him so much, which simply didn't make sense to her—not after her life, not after our lives; but isn't love, like God, inexplicable, a bond that transcends reason and sense? She still imagined, despite everything she'd heard, that he might snap out of his disease one day with the right medications, some new treatment.

Michael stood, got in the car. He didn't have any of his things. My mother, who saved everything and often reminded us what something we lost had cost her, didn't even ask about them. Something about the look on his face, the glazed-over eyes, warned her against it.

In the car, he told her everything. He told it to her clearly, miraculous for him, as if he were trying to hurt her, to blame her for what had happened.

Things had started fine. Michael thought that he had made two friends. He imagined, for a moment, that he was someone you could like. Even the thought of connection brought a lump to his throat. People feared Michael. People actually left the mall because of him. He was now the filthy beggar that bugs you at 7-Eleven, the guy with a WILL WORK

FOR FOOD sign sitting by the on-ramp that you make sure not to make eye contact with, a criminal.

They weren't his friends was how he began, my mother told me.

They—the three of them—had been watching a movie, a comedy. They were laughing. One put his hand on Michael's leg. Either one, doesn't matter. They were criminals. I'm not even giving them names. Michael heard the chattering, heard voices, but the medication turned them into whispers, indecipherable, distant things. The new, stronger medications smudged everything. And they also made him slower, uncoordinated.

He—one of them—kissed Michael's neck, licked his face. They were still laughing, really drunk. It was funny—those idiots, those fucking assholes on the tube, man, they were funny, right. Hand on a leg. Lights dim. Just laughing at those crass-ass motherfuckers cracking us the fuck up on the tube, right. Ain't trying nothing funny. No bullshit.

My brother sat blank-faced, tensed up, thought of Florida, of how painful it was to get fucked, because fucking, he knew, was a violent act, an act of power or acquiescence, fantasy or nightmare, depending on which side of it you were on.

For these two guys, my brother was someone who didn't matter, who would never matter, a guy the world would be better off without, so who would care if he was held down and fucked, fucked in his face and in his ass. Because he wasn't human, he was a plaything, a grotesque fuck-doll for crimi-nals, just like some of those geeks in juvie, the punks that the kingpins made grab their ankles and talk like a girl.

They'd been fucking boys in juvie, these two, had been fucked as boys in juvie. Boy, girl, didn't matter, just a hole, just something to shove your dick in, might as well be an animal, this fat ridiculous thing.

He let them do it. My brother didn't fight. Voices chat-tered. Maybe he left his body. I want to imagine that he left his body, a lot like S did the day he was murdered eight years earlier, and watched the whole thing with complete detach-ment, without a trace of pain or humiliation, with the beatific gaze of a saint or a department-store mannequin.

He didn't resist. He didn't resist when, in that blue blink-ing light from the TV, or God, whichever, they wrapped a bicycle chain around his neck. He didn't resist when they put their genitals in his face. He didn't resist when they tore his clothes and got him lying naked, rolls of flesh hanging off bone, his schizophrenic stink filling the house. He didn't resist any of it.

They did what they wanted, did everything, made him bleed, and maybe he thought of what hell might be like, just like this, living in a world where you did not matter, where nothing made sense and no one could be trusted, where every nightmare was physical, where you became a negative of what you once were and there was no help, anywhere, to be had.

—

The next day, after hearing the story, my father wanted to call the cops. But what could you charge against what amounted to, at least in a legal sense, consensual sex? My mother and Michael sat at the kitchen table as they had so many times before, silent. Michael seemed to be over it already, on to thinking of other things. My father locked himself in a room and broke things. When I heard the full extent of this story, years later, I locked myself in a room and broke things.

ASSISTANCE

After being raped by his two roommates,
Michael locked himself in his room and
prayed. He would act as if it never happened, then as if it was the only thing that
had ever happened. He told my mother to
die, that he was sorry; he came downstairs
and said he forgot what he was going to say
and then stared at the floor, looking for it, a
word crawling, an idea with a thousand legs.

His delusions intensified, delusions of
how evil the world was, of God as senseless,
deranged, torturous, full of love, full of hate.
God is all of these in the Bible, which, by
now, Michael had ingested, made a part of
himself, so his moods, I believe, were partially contingent on the tone of the verses

he had most recently reread. Ezekiel was contemplative. Job was broken and defeated. Paul was bristly and relentless. Mark was softer, hopeful and dreamy, but not without rage. Revelation brought on stark-raving fits.

There is madness throughout the Bible: the aforementioned Ezekiel has constant auditory and visual hallucinations; Nebuchadnezzar "ate grass as oxen for seven years"; miracles, resurrection, plagues, punishments; and of course there's John of Patmos' famous line: "He that hath an ear, let him hear what the Spirit sayeth . . ." Voices, visions. Nothing was real and everything was real.

Michael realized one day, while staring at his backwards self in the bathroom mirror, after a few hours spent with Revelation, that it wasn't God tricking him, but *them*, setting traps at every turn. He had his suspicions, had mentioned them to me that day in front of Robert Tilton, but now he knew. He withdrew for a few days, not answering knocks at the door, afraid to leave his room, filling the upstairs with a suffocating stink, then vanishing into a neurovegetative state, eyes sunk in his skull, fingers dangling, yellow and smoke-smelling, a corpse in a folding chair.

Then he woke as if from a dream into a fit of extreme paranoia, throwing open his door. What did you put in my food? Who hid my Bible? Goddamnmotherfuckingcocksuckingfuckingwhoremotherfucker.

Yellow teeth. Matted beard. Shouting with his head thrown back.

Let's just leave him alone, my mother would say. Just don't say anything.

It was 1991. Michael was twenty-four years old. He began to threaten my mother regularly—jokingly at first, but then for real. He became obsessed with fire, with hell and burning alive. He would look at her and quote scripture—usually from Revelation: "And upon her forehead was a name written, MYSTERY, BABYLON THE GREAT, THE MOTHER OF HARLOTS AND ABOMINATION OF THE EARTH . . . If therefore thou shalt not watch, I will come on thee as a thief, and thou shalt not know what hour I will come upon thee."

My mother, years later when I was badgering her with questions about Michael, told me that he used to hold a lighter up to her face while she drove him to the mall, saying that he would burn her if she didn't give him money, asking her if she knew what God did to stingy cunts.

He'd turn up heavy metal on the radio as they drove and say, I *dare* you to fucking touch that dial! Yet the next day, the next car ride, he might stare somberly and quietly out the window. He might tell her how much he loved her. You never knew.

His mood swings came and went like total eclipses. He would melt into sadness, mumble of suicide, of heaven. Then he would jump to violence, or at least the threat of violence. *Fuck off. Back off. Go to hell, cunt, cock, whore, asshole.* Confusion ate cankerous holes in his existence. He couldn't live at home anymore, said my mother, because now the threats didn't just seem real, they *were* real. This time she meant it, this really was the last straw in the ongoing line of last straws.

But you can't "put someone away" unless they've hurt another person or themselves. And even then the incident must be proven by law. Since "deinstitutionalization" took place in 1965 and psychiatric wards were cleared of all but the most severe cases, the number of lawyers in America has risen from about a quarter-million to well over a million. This means lawyers spawn at a rate of about four times the normal population, making them something, in reproductive terms, along the lines of unspayed cats. Innumerable lawsuits have been brought against states for housing the mentally ill. Many truly ill people have been sent out to be homeless, or to commit crimes out of desperation. A mother run through with a marine sword, a woman pushed in front of a subway train, two White House security guards gunned down, and so on—all possibly prevented with better mental health care.

It is a terrible thing, obviously, that mental patients have been mistreated, and it is something that has needed immediate addressing, but, like everything in America, the reaction has been absurdly, well, reactionary, making it in this day and age difficult for many families to help their own.

My brother went briefly into institutions a couple of times as both an outpatient and an inpatient between 1988 and early 1991. He once stayed the legal thirty days at a state institution west of the Blue Ridge Mountains. He went in, was heavily sedated, occasionally counseled, and thirty days later, according to Virginia Commonwealth law, he walked out, worse, and angrier, feeling *accused* of something and viewing his stay as simply punitive, his days filled with a regimen of minor punishments for breaking the rules and rewards for good behavior. This makes a schizoid personality further paranoid about the unfair state of the world, the fact that people are "out to get him."

My parents, however, would have thirty days of peace. They still had all their friends, but now spent most of their time at home, worrying, trying to figure out what to do with my brother. Kicking him out, or sending him away with money—any amount—wouldn't work anymore. He wouldn't *leave*. They were hostages to his illness, hostages in their own home.

My father, frightened of Michael now, would warn him often.

Do that again, he'd say about some strange behavior, some mean act, and you've got to leave, just pack your bags and get out.

Michael replied, on several occasions, that he'd murder us all if that happened.

My mother and father made endless phone calls, looking for anywhere that would take him, help him, keep him, feed him. They needed a referral, said the disembodied voices in the phone, needed to try other things first. They needed to bring Michael in for a pre-screening. They needed to call the police. My parents couldn't do it anymore. They couldn't afford it. They were going crazy themselves.

I sat in my filthy apartment, scraping up change to buy old paperbacks and quarts of cheap beer—usually malt liquor because it was stronger. I was skipping all of my classes, sure this was it, that I'd drop out. I ate rarely, ate nothing. I wanted not to care. We all wanted not to care for just a week, a day, an hour.

It wasn't quick, finding a place for him. It took time.

To make matters worse, Michael sensed the conspiracy, sensed that they were trying to get rid of him. He was right after all. No one loved him, no one cared about him.

—

On a sunny winter day—windy, cool but not cold—Michael was sitting outside in a lawn chair under the large open garage doorway, smoking, looking out onto the driveway, his hair down over his face.

My brother Ron and my father were washing the cars, talking, laughing. My father had told a dirty joke. Ron, fifteen, was shaking his head, saying how bad my father's jokes were.

My father sprayed Ron. Ron hit my father in the chest with a soapy sponge. They dodged water, screamed, giggled like children, ducking down behind the cars.

Michael picked up an aluminum softball bat that sat in a barrel, one of the replacements after the burning-cross ordeal, and held it in his lap. The voices were howling again. This new medication—there was always a new medication, a higher dosage—wasn't working. He could hear teeth chattering in his head that weren't his own. Something about the laughing stopped him from rocking silently and smoking.

They were laughing at him. That was it. There was real clarity—truth—in this thought. They were laughing at all that was wrong with him, laughing because they thought he belonged in a hospital, because they thought he was a faggot who liked getting fucked. They thought he was funny. They were spraying each other and throwing water and laughing and saying that Michael was an asshole, an idiot, a pansy, that he should die, that he should go back and live with those guys from the mall.

Ron did in fact hate Michael, as he told me on a number of occasions over the phone while I sat in my apartment trying to figure out what to say. He was young, and never knew what life was like without the insanity of Michael. My parents, particularly my father, who doted on Ron, went to great lengths to keep him away from Michael, to keep him active in sports (in which he was something of a prodigy) and school and always off with friends. Yet Ron once told me that he would like to kill Michael, finish everything, that even if he went to jail it'd be worth it, to get rid of that stupid bastard, and he was crying as he said this, a gentle kid, crying and wishing he had it in him to save everybody a lot of grief by killing his brother. I sat with the receiver to my ear, still only half-believing it had come to this.

Sometimes Ron made fun of Michael to his face. Ron had a temper, like my father and Michael, and, at moments, couldn't control it. When Michael pissed him off he'd let out a stream of insults, calling him a fat retard, a moron, a loser, a shit-smelling lard-ass.

Michael did, by appearances, seem almost stereotypically "retarded," mainly because paranoid schizophrenics care nothing for their appearance and lose all social sense of style; he wore pants a little too tight, shirts off the rack from Kmart, and sneakers years out of fashion; he also had his odd nervous habits of rocking and breathing in a long, loud, drawn-out way every few minutes. But I don't think his illness affected his intelligence at all; rather it bent otherwise normal, intelligent thoughts. Maybe he didn't get Ron's jokes, but insults he definitely understood.

Another symptom of schizophrenia—any book will tell you this—is the Oedipus complex: coveting your mother (in extreme cases, sexually); viewing your father as perhaps the source of all your demons, the head conspirator. This was true of Michael, particularly as he worsened with the years, as medication after medication after treatment failed to assuage his anxiety, sadness, anger. (Later I would read a marked-out, barely legible passage in Michael's Bible—1 Corinthians 5:1— in which Saint Paul wrote: "It is reported commonly that there is fornication among you, and such fornication as is not so much as named among the Gentiles, that one should have his father's wife.")

He didn't say anything the day of the car washing, Ron told me. There was no warning. He was sitting silently, as always, rocking, smoking, his lips moving whispered prayers or curses, and then he was up, chasing them through the yard with a fat-ended aluminum softball bat, huffing and running with a cigarette still in his mouth, swinging the bat through the air.

Our yard had a fence—six feet high, wooden, that my father had recently built to keep the neighbors from seeing Michael, from "knowing our business."

They were trapped in the backyard as Michael came at my father, swinging the bat wildly, cutting hard through the air, wanting to cave in his head. They were running around the yard, a sad suburban domestic scene you might have read about if it had turned out differently. Ron was a big kid, muscular, broad-faced and lean and heavy-shouldered like the rest of us, a national champion in freestyle wrestling, a thousand-yard rushing halfback. Which I believe was all that kept Michael from killing my father that day.

As Michael went at my father—*trying to kill him,* Ron told me—Ron tackled him from behind, tied up his legs and arms in a wrestling move, and began, by forcing Michael's head down and shoulders up in a full nelson, to try to suffocate him. Michael screamed, finally dropping the cigarette from his lips.

My father grabbed Ron by the shoulders and pulled him off Michael. My father was red with anger, brushing down his hair, telling Michael to get out of here.

Michael had gone from being lithe, muscular, and strong to being heavy and thoroughly out of shape. He'd almost died of starvation in Florida, returning skin and bones, then had regained all the weight quickly with his compulsive eating. He was weak now, without muscle or coordination, lethargic, unable even to throw a karate kick, his mental illness and the corrosive drug treatments eating away at him physically. Ron told me that he could have killed Michael. He felt in him the power to do so.

Michael went silently back into the garage to sit down and smoke. Episode over, forgotten. A minor scene in some sad lives. My father was sweating. He thought of calling the cops; then, looking at Michael lighting a cigarette, realized how embarrassing that would be, your own son coming at you with a softball bat. He didn't have the energy to explain anymore.

My mother, shortly after this incident, which augured what was to come, finally found a place to put Michael, a place where insurance would cover most of the cost.

It was an "adult community" in Williamsburg, an hour from our home, an apartment complex set back among rolling green hills and old trees, gates surrounding it. All of the tenants were mentally impaired in some way. Counselors were on duty twenty-four hours a day, and the patients were given the help psychologists deemed suitable—medication, counseling, work-study in some specific combination. It was a country club with a high gate.

Michael got to eat, sleep, sit out by a pool, smoke, read the Bible, and watch TV. All he had to do for these privileges was show up to counseling meetings, do one chore a week— dishes in the large disinfectant-smelling cafeteria, say, or weeding one of the mulch-covered gardens.

But he couldn't handle it. The voices, the paranoia, made it impossible somehow. The medications he was on at the time—Haldol, some sedatives to help him sleep, without which he would never have shut his eyes—just weren't enough. Nothing was enough. The weekly reports on him by counselors consistently said he was "difficult" and "uncooperative" and occasionally "aggressive in his behaviors."

He called home. No matter where he went, whether things were bad or good, he simply had to be with my mother. She was the only one he trusted, though he treated her worse than most people would treat a stray dog. She was the only one who had ever really shown him love, or even the slightest tenderness. He begged her: Please come pick me up. I can't stay here. I'm so lonely. You don't love me. No one loves me. I'll die here. They'll kill me, they'll eat my heart and take my soul.

My mother listened, cried while holding the phone. The voices were real, she knew, and the messages were real and the pain was real. Maybe the doctors could up the dosage of his medication. Maybe there was some surgery, even electo-convulsive therapy or ETC, commonly known as shock treatment. She'd heard of ETC, and maybe that was cruel, but what was crueler than watching him suffer like this?

My parents didn't sleep. They made phone calls. They took his phone calls, always the same, Please, God, come get me. I'm better now. I really feel pretty good.

Two, three in the morning, a phone ringing and ringing. My father in a chair, face sagging, eyes red. My mother pacing.

—

Michael came home every other Sunday. Counselors recommended this—"family time," they called it, "connection-making." My mother would go get him. She had to; he wouldn't get in the car with my father. He'd trundle out from behind the glass doors only if he saw my mother was alone. Michael had become certain that my father had something to do with the voices that muffled and confused the voice of God. My mother never even told my father about the lighter-flicking, the threats she tried to ignore, afraid that her husband would insist they completely abandon their son, which, despite everything, despite all this, was never an option for her.

I often went home on Sundays, the one night I ate a good meal. We all sat around somberly. The television droned through Redskins football games in the background. Throats gulped. My father's nose whistled. Michael rarely spoke. He ate loudly, and would have sent less hearty souls out of the room with all his slopping and belching, but we were used to it, could almost ignore it.

After dinner one evening, a few months into his stay at the adult community, both of my parents—not just my mother—took him back to his apartment.

It was dark. Michael sat in the back of the family van, edgy. He wouldn't sit down. He fidgeted. He lit a cigarette, put it out, lit another, started humming a church hymn, then singing it as loudly as possible. My mother would make sure to get Michael his "night" medication before the trip, a large dose of clonidine, a heavy sedative. This usually cut down on problems.

My father told him to sit down, to stop acting like this. My father's method was to act as if Michael were being ridiculous or childish. Grow up, he might say. Give me a break. For Christ's sake. *Unbelievable*.

Tonight nothing worked, no amount of talking, not even my mother's soft voice. He didn't want to go back, didn't want to live there.

While they were going forty-five on a secondary road, a back route from our home to Williamsburg, Michael opened the side door and jumped out into the darkness, tumbling into the grass, flipping and spinning and sliding down an embankment.

My father slammed on the brakes, screeching to a halt on the shoulder. In the side mirror, in the pinkish light of his brake lights thrown against the dark foliage of the woods, he saw the shadow of Michael take off running in a half-limp into the woods.

DEMONS

A state trooper found Michael early on the morning after he jumped from the van. He was walking along a road eight miles from where he had landed, hunched over, dragging his left leg along the gravel, disoriented, turning his head around to look at every car coming up behind him. He was cut, bruised badly down one leg, eyes blank, nearly in shock, mumbling. He couldn't remember his name. The trooper, making him stand by the car, shining his flashlight beam into his dead, black pupils, thought he was an overdose case, a kid strung out on PCP or crack or acid.

Michael knew that the trooper's badge was bugged, knew what the hissing whispers of the radio on his belt were saying about him. He knew the people in the cars slowing down to look at him were a part of all this. They were trying to trick him. They were trying to kill him. The trooper, my father, the nurses and doctors and grad-student counselors, everyone.

He put his hands on the hood of the car, spread his legs.

My father, after stopping the van the night before, under a bright moon-filled sky, had followed him into the woods on foot while my mother stayed put. But it was dark and my father was scared of Michael. Perhaps this was an ambush. Maybe Michael was waiting with a knife or a branch. My father hadn't forgotten the look in his eyes the day he wielded the softball bat, the way he would sit in a chair for hours, smiling, laughing, glaring at him, his own father. He had gone back to the van and driven to a pay phone, called the cops, then gone home and stayed up all night, waiting. He had made the right decision, he told himself. He'd done the right thing. Going into those woods after Michael would have been crazy.

—

Despite Michael's attempted escape, my parents took him back to assisted living in Williamsburg once he'd been released into their custody and taken to the hospital for a quick check-over (he had a few cuts and a sprained ankle; the ER doctors also thought he had overdosed on LSD because of his odd behavior).

My father refused to let him come home now, though he never confronted Michael with this. The cops at the small trooper station had been polite and seemed genuinely sorry for my parents. They sensed how troubled Michael was, and were somewhat surprised to see my parents come pick up a vagrant like him.

Michael wanted to go home, to live at home. But that was impossible. The cross-burning, the lighter-flicking, the threats, his endless rants followed by foul, dark moods, a dog so frightened of him she shook in corners when he entered a room, and, of course, the bat incident. He couldn't be trusted even to visit on Sundays anymore.

—

Michael realized, at assisted living, sitting in his filthy one-room apartment that people kept telling him to clean, watching Robert Tilton speak in tongues on a staticky old television, that the counselors were the pawns of my father, just like the doctors and nurses and probably that cop, too. My father made him come back here.

It was becoming clear. The medication was poison and meant to make his mind susceptible to infiltration by evil thoughts, to derail him from the straight track to God. Things were coming together. He was beginning to see that the face of God those many years ago, on the night I watched from the doorway, was a warning about the coming trials. It was written in Revelation 5:12, circled in Michael's Bible: "Saying with a loud voice, Worthy is the Lamb that was slain to receive power, and riches, and wisdom, and strength, and honor, and glory, and blessing." Michael was the Lamb. He had been slain long ago to receive the power of God. He was owed something. He would take it if he had to.

Food and clothing and wadded-up tissues and toilet paper filled his room. He blew his nose, childishly, on chairs, kicked the television. He spit phlegmy gobs into the carpet, where they baked in the afternoon sun. The smell was that of slow death; it seeped out into the shared, gated courtyard; other tenants—the thirty-year-old with Down's syndrome and the dwarf and the manic-depressive who'd tried to kill himself seven times—all began to complain of the smell, of Michael, or "Jesus," as they joked, ruining their community.

Below Michael's bed, in a dusty corner of the room, he made a tiny, intricately constructed shrine out of pills he should have been taking: yellow and blue and red, anti-psychotics and antidepressants and sleeping pills, aliphatic phenothiazines and thioxanthines and benzodiazepines, all stacked up like a rainbow pyramid at which to worship.

—

Counselors respected the privacy of the tenants, and only used their keys to enter rooms in cases of emergency. They tried talking to Michael through the door now, but he either didn't hear them or, more likely, couldn't make sense of what they were saying, especially now that he was entirely without any medication. They had already called my parents several times, but my parents couldn't do any better than psychologists and shrinks, they figured, so they didn't come up. The pattern was clear: When professionals can't help, they throw up their hands and send the severely ill person home or out into the streets.

Through the door, the voices told Michael he had to clean his room, that he couldn't live here—they always insisted it was a gift and pleasure to live here—if he didn't start following the rules, if he didn't adhere to the strict regiments dictated by the community agreement he had signed. Rule number one was be kind and respectful; number two, clean yourself; number three, clean your living quarters.

Bang bang bang. Michael.

As they knocked, he wasn't sure what he was hearing. Demons had been knocking at the door and window a lot lately and they were living in the pockets of his filthy pants, too, which he had just discovered the night before. He had stuffed the pants into the toilet to drown the demons, but he could still hear them whispering underwater. Sometimes he got on the floor to make sure the pills hadn't been taken by one of the invisible beings in the room with him. The flowers on the bathroom wallpaper were growing. Within the week they would have filled the room with unbreathable carbon dioxide.

Counselors liked to talk about "privacy." It was right up there with "healing" and "responsibility" and "trust" and "coming to terms" and "hope." But the smell was too much. Michael was too much. He constituted an emergency, a hygiene emergency, to be exact—rare, but they did happen among mentally ill populations, where a person, for instance, may see no reason to go to the bathroom anywhere but in his pants for days, may actually be *storing* the feces in his pants for one reason or another that is perfectly clear and sensible to him.

Using a key to gain access, two women swung open the door to Michael's apartment. The smell that met them literally almost knocked them off their feet. It was so bad they couldn't go in. It filled their sinuses, got stuck in the backs of their throats. They retreated quickly, leaving behind a janitor's cart full of cleaning materials outside his door. The other tenants stood around, trying to see in the door, all gaping mouths and puzzled looks.

In a place where mental impairment was the norm, Michael set new standards, forced them to make new rules.

He had put back on his underwear and a shirt. He was crying but he was laughing, too (much as he had done during other psychotic breaks), sitting on the bed, trying to catch his breath. The underwear was yellowish gray, his T-shirt had food stains on it. His gut hung out of the bottom of the shirt, over the waistband of the underwear. He glowed gray with his own sadness.

If they'd had any idea that he hadn't taken his medication for a week, they wouldn't have left all those cleaning fluids sitting there. However, they didn't usually deal with patients as risky and dangerous as Michael. He belonged in a locked ward with constant supervision. He needed to be secured for his own safety.

He stood up, looked at everyone, and said he'd clean the apartment. Tears were still rolling down his cheeks. The counselors, back now with a mop and their hands over their faces and mouths, said something about a reward, said something reassuring straight out of a manual.

Michael pulled the cart into the room, closed the door. He was going to cooperate; he shrugged, looked sheepish, which they took, wrongly, to mean he was sorry.

Thank you, they said. We'll check back shortly.

They tried to be positive. They had fangs in their mouths and microchips in their heads.

—

So maybe he began cleaning; maybe, just for a second, he'd pulled out of his psychotic state, pulled the pants out of the toilet, turned on the shower to rinse his waste down the drain. More likely, though, the demons were screaming, telling him what to do, what he had to do to get out of this mess.

Maybe God didn't love him. Maybe his parents and brothers didn't love him. He certainly had no friends. The people who mentioned his name did so shaking their heads. He was a lost kid, a lost cause. Crazy. But the demons were real, he knew that much. And God was real. He'd seen his face. He'd been chosen, but for what? Ever since the night of the Ozzy Osbourne concert, they'd been trying to trick him, to keep him from God, to break up the messages that were shot through space from the mouth of God into his brain by howling and hissing and laughing and accusing. His family was in on it. These counselors were in on it. The woman at the 7-Eleven where he bought cigarettes on special trips off the compound was in on it. Molly the dog was in on it. The President of the United States was surely in on it. CNN kept a camera aimed at his door. Robert Tilton could help, but now Michael didn't have any money to send him, and Robert would think that Michael had lost his faith.

And he had lost faith, and along with it the last traces of his will to live. On the bottle of Drano sitting on the bottom shelf of the cart, it said that it "cleared away," that it "cleansed," that it was "fast-acting." Standing in the center of the filthy room, in a stench he didn't even notice, he drank from the bottle of Drano, slowly at first, the harsh alkaline taste sending a shock to his brain, the smell collecting in his ears and nose and chest, overpowering, like fire behind his face, dancing up behind his eyes. Then he drank more, and faster, until he fell over backwards into a bright blue oblivion that felt better than anything had in a long, long time.

CONFESSION

After this suicide attempt, Michael had to have his stomach pumped and was in the hospital for two days. In a way, though, a way in which you may need this level of insanity in your family to understand, this was something of a blessing in disguise. Michael lived. We all cried, we all lost our minds a little more. But within a week he was back to himself, tattered, broken-souled, head full of God, but on his medication again. And now, because of the incident, because he had, according to the law, attempted to "commit harm to himself or another," he was committed to a local psychiatric home for adults, where he had to have a pass to leave, which meant he could not leave, period. It was called, somewhat euphemistically, a home for adults.

Finally he was in a place, we thought, where they could handle him. And this time he could stay, at least for a few months, maybe even a year. In the relative world of my family, Michael being locked up in a place with twenty-four-hour care and locked steel doors was a bit like winning the lottery.

For a long time I wished my brother had succeeded in killing himself, in snuffing out the last embers of his heart, in destroying all the misfiring synapses, or demons, in his mind. I didn't voice it, maybe not even to myself, because it seemed so hideously cruel and aberrant and frightening, but I felt it, this want, this secret wish for death and freedom, burning deep down inside me.

What does that mean—to wish someone dead whom a part of you still loves, whose memory haunts you like some illness in remission? I'm ashamed I felt that way now, but in the interest of honesty, of rendering something approximating Truth—as much as that is possible—that's how I felt then: disappointed he didn't finish the job. I'd like to say I was a different person from the one capable of these thoughts— I'd like to paint myself a stronger, more forgiving soul, to take more after my mother than my often angry father—but I wasn't.

I felt now, after this attempt, even more so than when I was a child, as if I were dreaming my life, dreaming this story of Michael as it unfolded. I felt as if my recent life were a bad movie, the memory of which I couldn't get out of my mind. My reality began to seem questionable, literally unbelievable.

Sometimes, when I'd be out in the world, out among people and friends, which was increasingly rare, I'd have to duck into a public rest room at a fast-food joint or a shopping mall, or go sit in my car because thoughts of Michael overtook me, though they didn't even seem like real thoughts, but rather thoughts based on, inspired by, movies or books or dreams—based on life, maybe, but not life itself.

In those days, in my early twenties, one minute I'd be fine, or what passed for fine then, and the next minute I'd be nauseous with anxiety and sadness, and I'd have this whole archive of filmlike memories and regrets to sift through before I could carry on to the next task of the day, which may have been simply turning off a light or putting a CD on or capping a pen.

I once, around this time, tried to break my hand by punching a brick wall, *just to feel some tangible, physical pain* (I quit after spraining my thumb and ripping the flesh off my knuckles). Years later, thinking of this act, the memory of which seemed suspect, I came across a book in a graduate-school library about mentally ill patients, usually women, for some reason, cutting themselves with razors as a way to test the bounds of their reality, to make sure they were actually *here,* that all this around them, this unfathomable world, was real.

I thought of going to a doctor, a shrink, but then I was afraid of someone officially telling me how messed up I was, because diagnosis, in my mind, would give how-messed-up-I-was a concrete name and a name would make it a fact, indisputable. My brother's insanity worsened once it had a name, once it was called schizophrenia—it then, it seemed to me, became something giant and solid and indisputable. I didn't want anyone giving the way I felt a name. My name for anxiety was "Michael." My sadness was called "family." The dangerous parts of living were called "love."

—

Michael's suicide attempt occurred in January of 1992. Three months later, I was sitting at the bar at my parents' house, drinking a beer. I'd grown my hair into a wild mane of curls, because I didn't have the energy for anything as banal as a haircut, wore the same filthy Atlanta Braves baseball hat every day to assuage how unkempt I was.

It was Saturday, the Easter season, sun shining, grass green, its scent heavy on a breeze blowing through the house. My parents were out.

Over the years my constantly working parents, raise by raise, promotion by promotion, had made improvements to the house: landscaping, new furniture, wooden flowerpots hanging below windows. We were solidly middle class: my father's great dream, to not have to be ashamed of his life and abilities.

I think we were all sure now that Michael would succeed in killing himself soon. Despite the fact that a part of me had secretly wished he'd succeeded with the Drano, I was petrified of him trying it again. Both my father and I were approaching breakdown. I believe my father would have fallen over the edge without my mother. I watched him on weekends when I visited, black-eyed from insomnia, quiet.

I was thinking about all these things—my father's depression, how much I was drinking nowadays, what seemed my brother's impending suicide, how my mother was the only one holding us all together—when the phone rang.

I usually didn't answer their phone—didn't even answer my own anymore—but today I picked it up. And in that split second, as the phone left the receiver and made its way to my ear and mouth, everything changed yet again.

It was Sergeant M from the Hampton police department. He wanted to know my relationship with Michael.

I'm his brother, I said, wanting to hang up, wanting more than anything not to have to hear what he had to say.

He asked if my mother or father was home, or if there was any number where he could reach them immediately. He then told me that Michael was in police custody for the murder and rape of S on June 10, 1983, in our old neighborhood. He said to have my father call him, he said thank you, and then he hung up. It was all very polite, very business-like. There was no more passion in his voice than in a phone solicitor's.

At first I just sat there, probably for a half hour or more, my thoughts as blank as they had ever been, the blood beating

in my temples. It was like I turned off. I couldn't think. After a
while I went into my parents' bathroom and vomited up beer
and bile. After that, I wondered if I had dreamed the whole
thing. There seemed a porous border between the actual and
the possible, the real and the imagined. And I hoped this had
taken place in the realm of the possible and the imagined,
that perhaps I'd been sucked into Michael and God and
Satan's void, an upside-down world where dreams were as
solid as stone. I wanted, for one fleeting moment, to have hal-
lucinated, to have broken through reality's delicate plane and
into the world of the insane.

—

On the day before the call from Sergeant M, my brother had
become convinced that the workers in the adult home were
working for the devil. The medication was poison. The inter-
com read his thoughts and the room was bugged. The heater
hissed threats. If he sat on the bed, demons would grab his
ankles and pull him under, straight into hell. He had no belt,
nothing sharp, no chemicals to drink. Twenty-four-hour sur-
veillance.

But there was routine. And Michael learned it.

On Monday afternoons the well-behaved patients were
allowed to go to the recreation area out back: an exercise
course with pull-up bars and various other workout equipment, a basketball court, and benches, just a few hundred
yards from an industrial park, less than half a mile from a resi-

dential area and strip malls. The benches filled with patients quickly because everyone was medicated, filled with light and heat, their thoughts just out of reach.

Michael was, I believe, taking his medication at this point because he was forced to. But medication only works to an extent for cases as severe as my brother's, the positive effects often diminishing over time. Then a new treatment procedure becomes necessary. And sometimes the treatments most effective to the mind become toxic to the body, poisoning the blood, swelling the kidneys and the bladder.

Michael wasn't really planning to escape, or perhaps "sneak away" is a better way of putting it. That, with taking the heavy sedatives, would have been far too sophisticated a mental undertaking. He had a head full of thoughts, memories, fantasies. They mixed together to form story-dreams that were, to him, real. He had crumbled under the world's many shifting meanings.

A part of how we survive has to do with our ability to accept the reality within which we live, and adhere to its basic rules of conduct. All religion and philosophy point us to this end or point out this end. This is the ultimate message of ideologies—religious, philosophic, scientific, consumer-based. Schizophrenia, however, destroys this innate human reasoning ability, our ability to literally *fit in,* and life thus becomes unacceptable on every level. You conclude, again and again, that you simply *do not matter*, so you begin to construct intricate mental worlds in which you not only matter but in which you are the epicenter. That is, of course, until some small chink of reality's light wrecks the delusion and those worlds crumble, as they always do, and others must be created. You need a signifier, as Dr. Smith would have put it, for why you don't matter, for the unbearable, seemingly sourceless oppression and persecution: the devil, your father, satellite messages, big government, the CIA, the president, the liberal media, minorities, lawyers, your own guilt, chemicals in cupcakes, the stock market, and so on.

During recreation hour on Monday April 13, 1992, Michael made his way over toward the main building of the home, waited until the two male psych nurses had turned around, and scaled a short fence that surrounded the building (this was not high-security in the least; most people here were addicts or depressives, no threat to anyone; even the schizophrenics besides Michael were less severe cases and for the most part docile, working toward living independently).

He landed on his feet, kept close to the building and out of sight of the workers. He walked away. It was easy. He strode through the city of Newport News, which borders Hampton, past old homes and convenience stores and Laundromats, under hissing power lines.

It was his fault, all of it, the whole world, the universe spinning endlessly away from God. My brother believed, today at least, that he had to pay for the world's sins with his own blood. That's what my father expected of him. He realized, though, that he shouldn't kill himself; that was a sin against God, a constant pull in his mind, but a mistake, impure, insuring certain damnation. He had to be killed by the state. He had to be made into a martyr for lost, murdered children by—and it made perfect, intricate sense to him—admitting he murdered one.

The death of S—he had seen the crime scene, studied its arrangements, the movements of the cops through the woods—was something preeminent in his mind, one of those thoughts that became confused with others, attached to others—things real, imagined, heard, read. To be a murderer, a child murderer, is to be defined, to have concrete meaning, to be the true godlike center of a world that does in fact make perfect, horrible sense. To be a murderer is to have a solid identity.

At a 7-Eleven, nine years after the murder and rape of S in our old neighborhood, Michael called 911 to confess his sin: He was the one. He was a rapist and murderer. Please come pick me up, he begged. He'd be waiting right here.

INFAMY

From the front page of *The Daily Press,*
Tuesday, April 14, 1992:

YEARS AFTER SLAYING,
MAN SURRENDERS

Almost nine years after police
found the partially clothed and
strangled body of a 13-year-old
Hampton boy, a 25-year-old Newport News man turned himself in
to police Monday. But he didn't
say why he waited so long.

Michael Scott Bottoms, of the
██████ block of Main Street, was
charged with murdering ███████
on June 10, 1983.

He is being held without bond in the Hampton jail, said Sgt. ███ M███████.

Although investigators interviewed more than 200 people at the time of the killing, Bottoms was never a suspect until he phoned police Monday morning and said he wanted to talk about the slaying, ██████ said.

██████'s partially clothed body was found a day after he disappeared in 1983 walking to a friend's house in Powhatan Park. He was discovered on the wooded path near what was then road construction for Powhatan Parkway extension. The area is now part of that road. An autopsy revealed that ██████ was sexually assaulted and strangled, apparently with one of his own socks.

An Eaton Junior High eighth-grader, ██████ probably died within 30 minutes after he left home that afternoon, police say. Bottoms was not interviewed during the investigation because he didn't live in the area, said ██████. Bottoms, 17 at the time, lived in Poquoson.

On Monday morning Bottoms phoned Newport News police from a Newport News business and said he wanted to talk about the case.

Newport News sent investigators and contacted Hampton police. "After the interview we had enough evidence to charge Bottoms," ██████ said.

Police refused to say whether Bottoms confessed to the crime and said he was not specific about his reasons for calling police. "They were not friends," ███████ said of Bottoms and the youth.

Police are also looking at other unsolved slayings to see if Bottoms might be connected, he said.

Bottoms is unemployed and lives with several people in a house in the Hilton area.

███████'s father, ███████████, said he didn't think Bottoms was a friend of his son's.

███████ said he was reluctant to speak about the arrest Monday: "I hope it's the guy. It's something that I want to make sure there are no mistakes."

It was big news. The sensationalism of it—the nine-year-old murder of a child solved—overwhelmed the lead of the news cycle for more than a week, my brother's name, *my* name, coming out of the television like a knife. His face, bloated and unshaven, shadowy and full of malice—a character seemingly special-ordered to run with an article about murder and rape—also filled the top half of the front page of the paper.

I saw the picture, but didn't, couldn't, read the story, couldn't muster the strength it would have taken to perform that monumental task. My hands were shaking. I couldn't even hold the paper.

I stared at his picture that day, into the eyes—black, empty, full of pain. I knew this was my brother, in a way, but, again, and especially now, it was all taking place at a certain remove. There was a part of me, a flash in my memory, that knew my real brother was just some kid, lost somewhere between this world and the next, still eight or nine years old, running through a front yard, holding a football, telling me to go long, go long, smiling with his crooked smile and gap teeth and wearing his favorite Levi's jean jacket. Could he be that person and this one? I wondered. Could, over time, this type of metamorphosis actually take place?

When I saw my brother's face—a mug shot complete with numbers—on the TV news for the first of many times that morning, I became violently ill from nerves. With that televised image it became real, out in the world, twisted and official, part of a collective knowledge and never, ever retractable. I was losing my mind a little and I believed, somehow, that by not reading the article in the paper I could keep this away from me. But not now, not with the television blaring my name into the room. Perceptions were made. Before I thought they—the cops, the media, the doctors, someone—would figure it out. Surely they would see the misunderstanding here, that the person they had in custody was insane, was having long talks with demons and angels, could put a cigarette out on his forearm with a deranged smile on his face.

The story was the lead on every local morning news program—murder solved. I remember very little of the day. I remember how I felt but I don't remember many of the specifics that triggered these feelings beyond the images of my brother. I sat on my parents' new couch, remote in hand. Aunts and uncles were there, my parents' friends, my grandmother, but they were like furniture to me; I could have been sitting there alone.

—

People brought food as if for a funeral. We watched television all day, waiting for the next news break, blank-faced, the phone ringing and ringing and none of us daring to answer it, knowing it was a journalist. Cars inched slowly around the circle in front of my parents' home. The phone wouldn't stop.

I think part of me believed it—murder wasn't beyond Michael. I remembered all the beatings, remembered his words: *Start the mower. Or I will kill you.* I went over the details of the time when the murder took place. He was seventeen in 1983, experimenting sexually. Since then he had had violent sexual encounters, both heterosexual and homosexual. I'm fairly certain he had participated in at least one rape while in Florida, and he had been raped at least twice. All of this, though, happened later.

It wasn't beyond him now to simply *say* he did it. His sensibility had shifted so drastically in the years since that time; 1983 would have been about the time he killed all his snakes, about the time he was at his most violent, at least toward me. I didn't know what to feel or how to respond. I was numb at the idea of Michael as a murderer, but then I thought, Of course, if anyone is a murderer it is my brother, and I am now the brother of a murderer and my life is over.

I'd seen him fold under sadness and confusion—moments that produced a great sadness and sympathy in me—but I'd also seen something in his eyes just before he threw me against a wall long ago, just before he let out a string of furious expletives at my mother, something dark and implacable. Maybe he did it, I thought. Maybe he didn't. For days after this, I weighed the pros and cons for his innocence and guilt, as the story in the local media took on a life of its own.

Anchors read the story at every news break; it was the top of the morning and noon news. As the day progressed, I started to become angry. How hard was it, I wondered, to find out and report that Michael was an acute paranoid schizophrenic who had just jumped the fence of a psychiatric-care facility? I didn't expect them to say he was innocent, to blow off a signed confession, but I did expect them to report *all* the facts. I just wanted someone—anyone—to mention that he was severely mentally ill.

"Bottoms is unemployed and lives with several people in a house in the Hilton area," wrote the reporter. For God's sake, I thought, he left a *nuthouse*. An unemployed man admitting to a murder and an acute paranoid schizophrenic who was AWOL from a psych ward admitting to a murder are different narratives indeed. The former is a better scoop, certainly, but leaving out the latter is almost—whether from incompetence or laziness or stringent deadlines or whatever—a subtle form of lying. I don't know what happened, don't know how that fact could have been left out of every story. Maybe the journalists didn't talk to the cops, or the cops didn't mention that one thing; maybe the journalists had a story and ran with it because it was a great story and their time to research it was limited; maybe they simply weren't competent; maybe someone in my family should have answered the phone and told whoever was on the other end how sick Michael was, how he'd drunk Drano, how he'd been homeless, how he heard messages from God in the Robert Tilton show.

Watching people talk about you on TV was like staring into a lake at your own reflection and watching it walk away as you stood there. At the end of each televised segment on my brother (fifteen seconds that felt like hours, that stretched out in elongated dream time), you would be convinced that he had been free and raping and murdering children for the last decade, his mug shot up in the corner of the screen, over the pretty anchor's shoulder, her expression momentarily serious before she changed moods, face breaking into a smile, for the great spring weather.

My father had gone down to the police station the night before, immediately after he and my mother had returned home and

I'd told him about my conversation with Sergeant M. Before he left, he looked at my younger brother, mother, and me and said that we needed to prepare ourselves. With glazed over eyes, he said—and I remember this perhaps more clearly than anything in my life—Michael may have done this. Then he turned around, picked up his car keys, and left.

When my father arrived at the station, Michael refused to talk to him. When he left, crying, someone outside took his picture, filling up his eyes with white-blue dots. That was one of the worst things, he told my mother, worrying about what would become of that picture, what story would run below the image of him with tears in his eyes.

—

From the local section of *The Daily Press,* Wednesday, April 15, 1992:

SUSPECT CALLED
SWEET, TROUBLED
NEWS OF MAN'S ARREST
ASTONISHES NEIGHBORS

The man who turned himself in Monday in the slaying of a 13-year-old boy almost nine years ago lived near the victim for several years and is remembered by neighbors as both "a wonderful sweet boy" and a troubled teen.

Six years before the slaying, Michael Scott Bottoms, now 25, lived with his family in the same Hampton Terrace subdivision as ▓▓▓▓▓▓▓▓▓. In 1983 ▓▓▓▓'s partially clothed body was found in a woods not far from the neighborhood.

"He had lived in that general area prior to the attack and was familiar with the area," Hampton Commonwealth's Attorney Christopher W. Hutton said Tuesday.

Bottoms, who moved to Poquoson with his family in late 1977, often returned to visit old friends and neighbors, sometimes staying overnight, several former neighbors say.

The news of Bottoms' arrest Monday, almost nine years after searchers found the boy's body, astonished some of Bottoms' former neighbors.

"It puzzled me because I never would have expected him," said Wesley R. Drew, a Prince James Drive resident, who lived a few doors from Bottoms and his family. "I've known him since he was a small boy. He always struck me as real nice. This is a big shock to me," Drew said.

Bottoms called Newport News police Monday morning, saying he wanted to talk about the June 10, 1983, unsolved Hampton murder. Newport News police interviewed Bottoms, then contacted Hampton detectives.

Bottoms, a resident of the ▮▮▮▮▮▮▮ Home for Adults [on] Main Street, was formally charged with murder at 1:40 P.M. A Hampton juvenile court judge Tuesday appointed local attorney Lacy L. Scoggin to represent Bottoms.

Scoggin declined to comment about the case and denied a request to allow his client to be interviewed. Bottoms remains in the Hampton jail without bond.

He faces a preliminary hearing in juvenile court on May 21, Hutton said.

A woman promptly hung up the telephone when the family home was called Tuesday.

Police declined to say why Bottoms decided to come forward after almost nine years.

Drew and three other former neighbors, who spoke on condition their names not be used, recalled Bottoms as a bright, playful young boy who wrestled on the same youth team, the Hampton Cubs, as ▮▮▮▮▮▮▮'s younger brother and swam at the neighborhood pool.

Drew said Bottoms used to ride three-wheel all-terrain vehicles with him and his children on the dirt paths that connected Hampton Terrace with the Powhatan Park subdivisions. The body was found near the site of the Powhatan Parkway highway extension.

"All the kids used to play there. We used to ride

our bikes on the trails and go hunt for snakes and lizards," said one former resident who lived a few doors from the Bottoms family.

City records indicate that the Bottomses lived on Prince James Drive in Hampton, about a block and a half from the ███████, from September 1965 until November 1977. Bottoms was a fourth-grader at Lee Elementary School about the time his family moved, a Hampton school official said.

Several of Bottoms' new neighbors on Rue Degrasse in Poquoson recalled Michael Bottoms as a troubled teen-ager who seemed lost.

"He was a wonderful sweet boy. I don't know what happened," one of the Poquoson neighbors said.

Hampton neighbors agreed that as a younger boy Bottoms was outgoing and friendly but he changed as a teen.

"He just wandered aimlessly. He apparently went to different places. After he moved to Poquoson he kept coming back, almost like he was lonely and missed it," a Hampton Terrace resident said. "He was getting to the point where he was becoming pathetic. He was obviously having trouble adjusting and had gotten in with the wrong crowd."

Bottoms graduated from Poquoson High School in 1986. Principal Don Bock said Bottoms was not pictured in the yearbook that year.

Police and court records show the only conviction against Bottoms was a minor traffic offense in York County in December 1984.

Some former neighbors questioned why Hampton detectives never questioned Bottoms earlier in the investigation. But Hampton police spokesman Sgt. ███ M███ said, "There was nothing in the beginning to lead us to him."

Sergeant M didn't understand my brother—how could he?—and I imagine he was the kind of guy—a good cop, a guy who went by the book—who believed there was no side beyond the obvious victim's, the poor kid—a thirteen-year-old, for God's sake—who'd been raped and murdered. They had good reason to think Michael was guilty. Even though my brother was raving mad at this point, his confession was elaborate and full of details "unknown to the general public."

When the two Newport News police officers answering the call on Monday, April 13, had spoken to Michael outside of the 7-Eleven, where he waited for an hour for them to arrive and arrest him, they thought it was a prank; they thought, in fact, that he was homeless. They smiled at Michael and one even told him he should just go home now, that calling the police department was not a joke and there were actually penalties for that, including jail time.

Then Michael told them he could prove his guilt. He begged them to believe he was a murderer. He would show them. They listened, saw the absolute sincerity in his face, the way he stared at the ground, embarrassed, blinking back tears, and then they took him to the Hampton police department. Once there, my brother not only confessed; he bolstered his confession by offering a wide range of intricate circumstantial evidence against himself. He made it nearly impossible for the police not to believe him.

—

The old neighborhood had changed. A highway cleaved the forest where I used to play, where S was found. Traffic roared where woods once were. New subdivisions had sprung up over the years, each house a near replica of the next.

My brother, in the backseat, had guided Sergeant M and his partner through the city in a brown unmarked Aries K car (in my imagination, all detectives drive these cars), past malls and fast-food joints, under billboards, into and out of the smell of processing plants and seafood plants and shipbuilding yards and government housing projects. Sergeant M and his partner listened, bewildered, only half believing it was worth their time, neither of them completely familiar, yet, with the old murder. It didn't help that Michael looked like such a stereotypical lunatic.

But my brother insisted. He took them to the exact spot where the body was found, told them how it had happened, what he had done. He had used a sock. There were clothes, a shirt over there, on a branch. He had liked doing it; at first he didn't think he could, you know, really kill someone, really send his soul on to the next world, but when he did it, man, he felt a hundred feet tall and made of nothing but blood and muscle. He told them how snakes ate mice and it was like they were absorbing their essence. They stared at him.

They took in the show, his unbelievable insistence. He was obviously unstable, probably just bullshitting. But they took him back to the station anyway, just to be sure, to check, even though crazies admitted to stuff like this at least a few times a year.

Later that afternoon, Michael sat in an office at the police station. He smoked cigarette after cigarette, going through a pack in a couple of hours, asking for another, rocking, the room filling with smoke. He sat by himself, the door closed, mumbling, moving his lips to form words, tapping his feet, rubbing his hands through his hair, exhaling in exaggerated bursts.

And the cops must have searched through computer files—or, better yet, they went digging through old file cabinets, like Kojak used to, like Baretta used to, in manila folders, trying to figure this out. Somebody. A kid, maybe eleven, twelve. No, thirteen. S. June 10, 1983. Sexual assault after the fact. Some seriously fucked-up stuff. Sodomy. First- or second-degree murder. Unsolved.

Sergeant M began matching the story he had just been told with the known facts of the case in the old, dusty folder. Every one matched, right down to exact location, wounds, the positioning of the body, the color of the sock. The officers couldn't believe it. The whole thing, the fact that Michael had decided to call from a 7-Eleven, was the stuff of legend, of late-night, booze-filled stories with other officers. You just didn't get this lucky in police work. That should have been their first clue that something was amiss.

They moved Michael to a private cell.

The phone rang at my parents' house while I sat, alone, drinking a beer.

Hello, I said.

⎯

I gave up my apartment and stayed at my parents' house during the four months that Michael was awaiting trial for the murder of S. He was moved to a psychiatric hospital, two hours west of Hampton. The information had finally sunk in with the police that he was schizophrenic once my mother produced documentation, though this information, once proven, didn't change the fact that Michael knew far more than he should about the murder. And there had been cases of paranoid schizophrenics killing neighbors, roommates, friends, their entire families. If anything, his illness made him fit the profile even better.

My mother and my father spent many afternoons with his public defender, discussing his illness, the case against him, quietly wondering if they shouldn't take out a loan to get another attorney, someone with more experience.

My mother, by now, knew her son hadn't done it. When she asked him over the phone why he had admitted to the murder, he'd said, Dad thinks I did it.

She said, No, Michael, Dad doesn't think that. Dad loves you. You didn't do this.

Dad thinks I did, he said. I know he does. He thinks I'm a murderer. He thinks I'm a very bad person.

She was hoping that everything would be found out and that this, finally, would be enough to have him institutionalized in a state facility. But getting through this wasn't going to be easy.

I couldn't sleep. I didn't eat. I lost fifteen pounds, my clothes hanging off me. I dropped all pretense of attending university, briefly took a job landscaping, thinking the hard work would do me good, get my mind off things, but I quit when the boss said my name sounded *really familiar* to him, that he'd heard it somewhere recently—not the kind of name you forget—and if he thought of where, he'd let me know.

I stayed in Michael's room, the only room with a bed upstairs, because mine had been turned into a den. I lived out of a single duffel bag full of books and jeans and T-shirts. I stayed up all night some nights, my eyes a couple of circles stubbed out into my head, reading, listening to music. Not only could I not eat, but now I had insomnia. I spoke to no one but my family and a few friends. The case was in limbo. They would keep Michael until DNA tests came back, then proceed accordingly.

Journalists called constantly in the first few weeks, hundreds of calls in a day. We let the answering machine catch everything. I often wish that I had spoken, that I had had the nerve to explain his illness, his delusions, but I didn't. And what if he'd done it? Unlike my mother, I wasn't at all sure he was innocent. Not yet, anyway. Was I willing to try to justify him, if a part of me doubted his innocence, if a part of me had always feared that he was capable of just such a grisly act?

⎯

I found Michael's Bible in a drawer of his desk one night. Over the next few weeks I read the New Testament, beginning to end, twice. He had written things in the margins, particularly those of Corinthians and Revelation. Sometimes there was just one word: PAST or FATHER or LUXURY. Other times, fragments of sentences: PATH TO GLORY IS SACRIFICE, DEATH IS BEGINNING. It was hard to make sense of it; it was muddled, sloppy, haphazard. No narrative arose in the margins, but I often read passages within the Bible text that I thought might have elicited his response.

According to Kierkegaard, it is only when one has lost everything, has been defeated so utterly by life that he can no longer function, that he might, from the true bottom of his existence, make a bid for Christian faith and the hope of salvation through the teachings of Christ. Michael and I found an interest in God in the same way: from looking up out of the bottom of our existence, two losers making a last bid for meaning.

I was stunned by the Bible on my first reading, how poetic it was, especially the Gospel of John and the Song of Solomon and Revelation; and how cautionary, how packed with tragedy and sacrifice. It was full of brutality and taboos. It seemed open to endless interpretation. Every passage was terse on the page but expansively aphoristic when you stopped and thought about it. I found it funny that anyone would profess to *know* the full meaning of it, especially someone as evidently dense as, say, Robert Tilton.

"And immediately I was in the spirit," begins a passage, "and, behold, a throne was set in heaven, and one sat on the throne. And he that sat was to look upon like a jasper and sardine stone: and there was a rainbow round about the throne, in sight like unto an emerald." (Revelation 4: 2–3) It struck me as astoundingly beautiful and creepy at once. I needed to know this stuff, it was where Michael was coming from. It was metaphorical to such an extreme that it seemed at times inscrutable, leading you toward ideal or Platonic truths, like Romantic poetry or even the more abstruse passages of Joyce, but not literal truth. It made me think that the small number of Christians I had listened to didn't know what the hell they were talking about, were in fact so ignorant of the book they professed to know and live by that I felt offended.

The Bible was by turns preposterous, entertaining, and profound. It was weird and beautiful, dated and new, murky and clear, sometimes on the same page. It felt like the truth in some way—it still does—but read like a fairy tale. I read and reread the Gospels of Christ in my schizophrenic brother's seared-smelling room. I sat in an old chair and looked at his posters—Bruce Lee was still up, as was the *American Pop* film poster. There was the aquarium where the snakes had lived, the window where God's face had shone. It was all here, his life was all here, and I wanted more than anything to understand it, to see it from the inside, no matter the cost.

I never visited him at the psychiatric hospital. I was too frightened, embarrassed, unconvinced of his innocence, paralyzed in my own disbelief and belief. But during this time I got to know him, as much as one could know Michael. I began to understand how he thought, how his mind worked, and where the essence of many of his thoughts came from, through reading scripture. I began then to try to understand his demise, and still later I tried to understand the facts of his disease, the sickness itself, through the metaphors of Christianity. I began to believe wholeheartedly in the existence of the Soul, because I needed to. I began to believe in the power of forgiveness and in the humble place of the individual in a grander, unknowable scheme. I began to believe in God in my own, very personal, way and to understand not only the power but the necessity of forgiveness.

It was all here, ready to be unlocked. The Gospels of Christ spoke of the ills of judgment, the necessity of humility, the frailty and sanctity of all human life. Jesus was a seditious radical of the first order. He was sorrowful and full of rage for this life; he buzzed with an intense humanity. He loved everyone, forgave everyone, and these thoughts, in this world, *are* radical. His people were the sick, the broken, the deranged—whores and lepers and orphans and thieves and, I suspect, the insane—those who went through life in pain, unloved, and he took them in, all of them, and, wiping their tears away, he said, You are my brother.

⸺

Michael was in the psychiatric hospital for four months and six days. My parents visited him once a week or so, and usually he didn't speak; sometimes he wouldn't even look up from the floor as he sat in an orange plastic chair in the middle of a white room. My mother asked the nurse if he was taking his medication, which he was, but he refused showers (he said he didn't trust the water).

It took all of my parents' strength to get out of bed on the days they were to go there. Every time they drove into the compound, they were afraid of being attacked by journalists, though journalists were never there because it was surrounded by a gate and security guards.

This was all unbelievable, beyond imagining, that this had become their lives, driving past guards and through high, gray metal security gates, but every day there it was—a fact: Their son had admitted to a particularly heinous murder and rape of a child; everyone knew their name.

In the third month of Michael's incarceration he was put in a new, private cell with a bunk bed. He was glad to be alone. In his private cell, he took off his orange standard-issue overalls, tied the left leg of the overalls around his neck, the right leg to the top of his bunk bed, and attempted to hang himself. A guard found him just after he had passed out, naked except for his underwear. Another minute would have killed him. Michael's knees were on the ground and he did it by simply falling forward, his sheer will to die.

The next day a facility psychiatrist prescribed a new psychotropic drug and stronger antidepressants. A week after the new prescription, Michael told the guards he had just been kidding, that he didn't really kill S, and he didn't know who did. He said he'd like to have his mother pick him up now.

—

Three weeks later, the DNA tests came back. As I've said, there had been a lot of evidence at the scene of the crime: skin, blood, semen, hair. The murder itself seemed unplanned, a scene of reckless carnage and brutality. The test results concluded that it was impossible that my brother had killed or sexually molested S.

During two psychological evaluations while in the hospital, Michael couldn't name the president, the year, or his date of birth. Yet he could remember every detail of the crime, down to the color of the sock used to strangle S. He could also remember things my father had said to him when he was a child, the kind of petty cruelties most of us are lucky enough to forget. From sparse details, memory, and continuous emotional trauma, he had created a wholly credible memory of himself as rapist and murderer. Then he remembered, a little late, that it was possibly a false memory.

When my parents went to pick him up, petrified, my mother shaking—once again, the state set him free, and free meant home—he recanted his innocence. As he walked down the hallway toward the outside and the waiting car, he insisted, despite the evidence, that he had done it. He then went on to explain how he had come up behind S in the woods, how S's breath was fast and hard, and he had strangled and raped him.

—

Nothing appeared in the paper about Michael's exoneration and release, the fact that he had invented the whole thing. I looked for this, and I've gone back through archives since then. Nothing. For years, when I saw people from my past while visiting my mother, I could always tell that they wanted, more than anything, to ask me about my brother the murderer, who had been released on one of those terrible technical legal glitches that entire television shows are based upon. Once you've been branded guilty by the press, you're guilty, period, despite any evidence to the contrary. If I didn't know this before, I know it now.

ABSENCE

Here's one for the absence-of-God argument, for life as absurd and lacking in all evidence of divinity and never adhering to a tidy plot. Here is the kind of narrative curve, lachrymose and violently cruel, that makes me doubt.

My father had been having pains in his side for some time. He had been so preoccupied with Michael that he hadn't gone to the doctor in years. Now, since Michael's life was in a temporary lull because of the near-toxic dose of antipsychotics he had been prescribed after leaving the state psychiatric hospital, my father visited a physician, who listened to his raspy chest, and sent him on to a specialist.

There were X rays, blood tests, MRIs, CAT scans, stool samples, a complete physical. What they found was a death sentence: a grapefruit-sized tumor in the lower lobe of his left lung.

He went into the hospital immediately for an emergency operation to remove the mass, and spent several weeks there recuperating, my mother, Ron, and I beyond shock now—feeling jinxed, hexed, at the wrong end of some karmic debt, three sad Jobs waiting for the next pestilence, the next wrath—sitting in my father's hospital room until late every night, and the strange thing—strange to me, considering the rage I felt—is that I bowed my head and prayed.

My father was diagnosed with malignant mesothelioma, lung cancer caused by asbestos, that brilliant and cheap American industrial insulation of midcentury used so generously in our "strategically sound location" for a home. He had contracted the disease while working at the Newport News shipyard for thirty years, punching a clock to pay our bills, to support *me*, watching his life slip past.

He'd probably inhaled the toxic fibers sometime in the seventies. Sometimes, doctors said, the disease sits dormant for years, until very old age (my father was fifty-one and in good physical shape); stress, though, brings down the body's natural defenses. Do you live under much stress, Mr. Bottoms?

My father went home from the hospital to die. While he still had strength—the first six months or so—my parents forgot about Michael, or tried to (they had relatives come by to talk to him while he sat and smoked, to make sure he took all of his new, stronger pills), and took a couple of short trips, blowing money on fancy restaurants and fine wine. But malignant mesothelioma is inevitably fatal.

My father had, the doctors said, maybe two years to live. The approach to this kind of thing was mainly pain management and containment. My mother and I bought him shark cartilage and bottles and bottles of pills—supplements, root extracts, condensed herbs, anything we heard about. We read every book on the disease, rented videos, investigated highly experimental procedures and checked about centers for last-chance patients, but those places are for charity cases or for the wealthy, and we were middlebrow, middle American, middle class. We had to solve our own problems.

After the short trips during the time when he still had a little strength, he became so sick that mostly he sat on the couch and whispered, stopped eating, and stared at the TV. He had a box on his hip and a catheter stuck through his side and into his lung that pumped a light dose of chemo through his body at regular intervals. After a few months he began to react to this medicine as if it were poison.

I've mourned my father a great deal over the six years since his death, though our relationship, during his life, was strained. I didn't really know him, the way I know my wife or good friends, the way I know my mother.

He took care of me, loved me as his son; I loved him as my father. And I believe these different loves, his and mine, were absolutely sincere and real, if perfunctory and distant and safe. But they existed within rigidly defined parameters. To reveal your true feelings was a breach, a way, he remembered from his own father, of opening yourself up to unbearable assault (he could still hear his father's voice some nights when he couldn't sleep, telling him how stupid his ideas were, how he got the son he deserved). We got along like colleagues working on vaguely the same project—our life—but at different ends, to stretch the metaphor, of the office. I learned how to stay out of his way. We acted as if we were both afraid of being rejected by the other, and acting this way meant that on some level we had been rejected by the other.

Four years after I watched my father die on morphine in his own bed, my mother gave me several letters he had written me through my life but had not given me. Most of them were dated in the mid-eighties, when I was a teenager. She had found them in a drawer. They were written in faded pencil, on yellow legal paper, with formal beginnings: Dear Greg, or, Dear Son. Many of the words were misspelled, sentences ran on. He told me in writing how proud he was of me, how I was a goodhearted person, smart, special. He said he worried that I thought about the bad things too much, that I was "too soft," too contemplative, spent too much time quiet and alone. He wrote in big, blocky letters, like a schoolboy sending a secret to a friend, that he loved me very, very much, always had and always would, that he saw good things in me, that if I worked I could probably go to college and have opportunities he never had. In a couple of the latest letters, he said to try to avoid thinking about Michael (these were dated long before the false murder admission), that he would be out of our lives soon enough, one way or another.

He implied that to live any kind of life I had to get away from here, away from all this accidental wreckage. Look forward, he wrote; don't dwell on all this. Never squander your dreams. Since I've squandered mine, sometimes I'm hard on everybody else's. I don't mean to be, he wrote. He loved me so much, he wrote. But he hated saying things like that because he "sounded like a jerk!" It was weird to say something like that to another grown man, or almost grown man. It was just easier to write things down and never show them to anyone. Like me, my father knew that the most dangerous thing was to love openly.

—

My father's illness more or less sent me over the edge. He was at home now, there was nothing more the doctors or a hospital could do, so I fled, which has always been my impulse, though I never completely succeed at doing this. At twenty-two, I decided I wanted to quit life. I had recently read *Walden,* and most of the curmudgeonly books of Edward Abbey, and the idea of living alone, away from everyone, away from these highways and shopping malls and suburban homes and kids and families, was alluring.

A friend from college was working for a guy outside of Rocky Mount, North Carolina, a couple of hours away, restoring a nineteenth-century plantation house. He asked, because of my brother and the whole fiasco, if I wanted a job for the fall and winter, wanted to get away from it all, live in a tent, get high and scrape old paint and sand boards and caulk windows. I would have said yes to anything. It gave me an excuse— work—to leave all my problems, to abandon my dying father and my brother, whose manic behavior seemed temporarily controlled, or almost controlled, by the new medications.

—

North Carolina was a haze. It was long days of work through cold, blue mornings and crisp, sunny afternoons, stoned, standing up on makeshift scaffolding made of aluminum ladders and bungee cords, pliant and unstable, holding a heavy sander to blast lead-based paint off a giant, old house, the owners of which were absent. By midmorning each day I was white with paint dust, as if dipped in flour, needing to change the filter in my respirator.

The work was hours disappearing, the sun sliding like a drop of water down the sky. I spent whole days performing the same motion: a sander back and forth, a paint scraper hacking away at what seemed like the same shutter, though by nightfall I'd have finished them all, without remembering exactly when one ended and the next began. I was thankful to have somehow missed a whole day.

At night, which fell like a stage curtain at five in those cold months, we slept in separate high-tech Arctic tents set up in the empty living room of the giant house, among boards, wiring, stacks of wallboard, tools, and rodent turds.

When my friend and I received a payment—a lump of cash, maybe a hundred bucks for my friend and me to split while the "boss" went to Greenville to stay with a girl he knew who kept breaking his heart—we'd go to a Mexican restaurant, drink margaritas and beer and laugh and make a commotion and I'd look at other families and feel like fucking crying. We'd blow all but gas money for the next week, and I didn't care. We'd wake up with hangovers like a ballpeen hammer to the forehead. Once we got tattoos. Another time we bought two ounces of pot to make sure we'd have weed to smoke (we decided it was better to be broke *with* pot than have money without it). We talked about Darwin and the Big Bang and God and the stranger fundamentalists in the news and how we both viewed organized Christianity as based upon the repression of pleasure. We spoke like the high, half-intelligent pseudo-bohemians we were.

I realize that it was here, on a plantation in the middle of endless North Carolina fields and farms, that I truly hit bottom, that the pressures of life began to seem too ridiculous to continue dealing with. It felt as if this was the beginning of the final act of some drama I could not control.

The most important thing for me in those months, after my brother left the state psychiatric lockup and my father was diagnosed with terminal cancer, was to be numb at all times, drunk or high and alone as much as possible. I thought of killing myself, pondered it in a philosophical way—weighed its pros and cons—but my aversion to violence, my astounding cowardice in the face of all physical pain, kept me from making any rash decisions. I was just so tired. I wanted to sleep and never wake up. I wanted to vanish and never be heard from again.

When the boss came back from the girl-who-broke-his-heart's house on Monday morning, February 22, 1993, he told me that my mother had called. Usually I called home on Sundays, collect from a pay phone outside a Rocky Mount Piggly Wiggly grocery, where I imagine the locals thought I was a hitchhiker, a vagrant. I had given my mother my boss's girlfriend's number, in case of emergency, which seemed, given the circumstances at home, always likely. My boss didn't know the details or the degree of damage, but there had been a fire. Everyone was okay. That was all he knew.

I borrowed five dollars for gas, got in my old station wagon, and left. My car shimmied along highways cutting through East Carolina fields that stretched out, golden and dead, to the hem of the sky. By the time I got home, late that morning, my brother Michael was in police custody.

INTENT

Michael ended this, his short, sad history
of life out in the world, on a cloak-black
morning during the coldest part of winter.
Heating units humming through the neighborhood, windows locked and full of clear,
cold sky.

Michael sat in a lawn chair in the garage,
looking at the floor, waiting. He couldn't
sleep, hadn't slept in days. In the last several
weeks, while I was in North Carolina, he'd
adjusted to his new dosage of psychotropic
medications that had been prescribed to
keep him calm after his release from the
state psychiatric hospital. He'd grown back
into his anguished self like a cloven worm.
For months after his false admission, his
thoughts had been smudged and indistinct,

his bloated body heavy and almost immovable; hallucinations hung to the periphery.

Now, though, his world flowered again—intricate conspiracies of emotion, good and evil, God and Satan. They were trying to steal his soul. There was a bug in his head that had been planted while he was under observation at the hospital, which my father had told the guards to put there while he was asleep from all those fucking pills. He thought there might be poison in the air, released to make his skin itch and break out. He rocked, smoked, chanted, prayed. He was back, and even worse.

My father was getting weak now from the chemo. In the last few weeks, every day had seemed a possible disaster, my father cutting his eyes at Michael to check his location, to make sure he didn't sneak up behind him. He told my mother he couldn't take watching his back at home all day, said his nerves were going to kill him faster than the cancer. You shouldn't have to be frightened in your own house. He and Michael, he said, circled each other like angry dogs waiting for an opening at the neck.

He had dreams of Michael shoving a knife into his chest and twisting it while he napped, which he literally could not help now. Dreams of ropes looped around his neck, shotgun blasts up against his face, dreams of Michael eating his flesh like a wild animal.

My mother kept looking for psychiatric treatment, a hospital, a group home, a supervised halfway house, a new drug.

She was diligent about helping him, helping us, to the end. Just when she'd find a place, get ready to sign the papers to send him off somewhere, she'd realize that even with insurance and his disability status, the cost would be several thousand a month, well beyond what they were capable of paying. She wrote letters to the state, letters to whoever would listen, wrote that in the last few years "Michael had become extremely dangerous to both himself and others," trying to mimic the legal language that kept tripping her up.

My parents and younger brother slept each night with locked doors as Michael now took to stalking through halls and rooms at all hours, listening up against doors, playing the TV at full volume.

My mother would sleep only an hour or two a night, listening to his footsteps in the hallway, hearing him stop in front of their bedroom door, whispering something, some prayer, some curse, much of which, she said, didn't even sound like it was in English.

The night of February 22, Michael put fifteen tablespoons of instant coffee into a mason jar full of water and boiled it in the microwave. He added fifteen tablespoons of sugar and a splash of milk (always fifteen and always Folger's for this ritual). He stirred it with a metal spoon, clinking the glass nearly hard enough to break it, pacing, bowing his head, saying Amen, going back to stir again, harder. He was electric, charged. He was an angel and the more coffee he drank the more powerful he felt.

The green digits on the microwave read **300**, which he read as **600**.

—

Michael had called my grandmother the day before to tell her he loved her and that he had a plan, something really big that would dramatically change the difficulties of the world, the course of history and suffering. Alarmed, but acting nonchalant, she asked what it was.

A secret, he said. He said that he was just waiting for them to tell him what to do, when to do it.

She tried to get him to talk. I love secrets, she said.

He told her she'd know when it happened; oh, she'd know, all right, and things would be a lot better for both of them. He said he'd like to come live with her maybe, so they could both stay up late and watch TV, watch David Letterman and do puzzles and drink coffee and smoke cigarettes, because Dad, he said, because *Dad* hates it when I turn up the TV at night. Then he hung up.

My grandmother called my mother at work. They had to get him out of the house now, she said. Michael was going to do something. He was talking nonsense about some mysterious they. Just call the police, she insisted. You need to call the police to let them know to watch out.

We can't, my mother said. He hasn't done anything and he won't leave. If we kick him out, he'll just come back.

—

Michael's plan was simple. He was going to burn our father alive before the demons completely overtook his soul. He believed our father would kill our mother by strangling her one night in bed; he had seen this in a vision given to him in a dream by a mysterious force named Utok the Angel, who didn't have a body but was instead pure energy and translucent, a wave of colorless movement speeding about in his room.

The same angel, in a different dream, told Michael that the bug in his head, a tiny metal transistor, had been planted by his father and was to keep Michael from interfering, to always know his whereabouts in the house. His father was the origin of all the voices. His father had made Michael a prisoner. Michael had finally been given full disclosure from the other world, the real world of dreams. All the tricks, all the lies, all the pain he had suffered and nightmares he had endured, were radiating from the center of his father's head. The whole cancer thing was an obvious ploy, more tricks, a way of getting Michael to drop his defenses in what had become a silent war.

Kill that motherfucker, Utok had said. It's the only way.

His father was flooding the world with demons, so no matter where Michael went, the forces of evil could squeeze through window frames and up through vents and along corridors, always shadowing him, always oppressing him. His father controlled the sewer systems and the radio towers and the satellite dishes in space. He controlled the demons and the demons controlled the world and that made our dying father the true nemesis of God, the Antichrist. That had been the message in the window when he was fourteen, only he hadn't known enough scripture then to read it correctly. The demons would always find Michael as long as his father was alive, acting sick, acting *innocent*, scooting around in his underwear with that ridiculous chemo tube stuck in his side.

Michael waited in the garage, smoking—he had to smoke in the garage now that his father was dying of lung cancer, further reason to hate him—until 4:30 A.M. He had set an alarm on a small digital clock that sat on a work-bench. Then he put out his cigarette and began to pray. The voices were becoming clear, but soon, if it all worked out, they would vanish forever with his father, vanish into oblivion with all evil. There would be light, a new world. *Blessed are they that do his commandments, that they may have right to the tree of life, and may enter in through the gates into the city. For without are dogs, and sorcerers, and whoremongers, and murderers, and idolaters, and whosoever loveth and maketh a lie.*

First he went upstairs, to my younger brother's room, which was locked. He lifted the smoke alarm off the small hook on the wall and put it in his coat pocket. On the stairs, coming down, he tried to be quiet, but some of the boards squeaked under his weight. My father heard him, but his stalking was normal. My father wheezed at night, couldn't sleep in certain positions because of the fluid that stayed in his lungs. He ignored the noise.

Michael went to the hall adjacent the living room. The smoke detector there wouldn't pop off the wall like the one upstairs, so he twisted the white cover until it broke off, then ripped the wires out, putting it all in his pocket. He took both detectors and threw one in the kitchen trash can and one in the bathroom trash can.

Now he went back to the garage. The good voices, the ones from God, were telling him what to do. The bad voices, those radiating from my dying father's head, were trying to trick him into stopping now while he still could, before anyone was hurt, before anyone was dead. They were saying bullshit things like his family loved him and that what was wrong was wrong with him. He *knew* he was right. The message was through an angel, from God himself. He wouldn't be tricked, not this time. He knew what he had to do, knew he had to kill his family to be free and to set them free. To murder was to free the soul from its cage, from pain and hopelessness, a noble, godly deed. In his mind he was doing my family a favor. They would never be lonely or afraid or worried again. They would never fight or yell or cry or sit quietly and gloomily in that somber house. They would know only love and God's grace and forgiveness. They would go to heaven, maybe even my father, too, if God found it in his heart to forgive him. They would lose their bodies and live forever.

Picking up the gas can, he headed back into the house. It was now ten after five. At the bottom of the stairs, in front of my parents' room, he poured a pool of gasoline on the floor. He held the can close to the ground to quiet the splash. He lit a wooden match on his zipper, tossed it into the pool of gasoline, and watched the rising breath of flames. Heat radiated in concentric circles past him. He waited a few seconds to make sure it closed off the doorway in fire, then headed back to the garage.

In the garage he dumped the rest of the gasoline around, splashing it on the floor and up over his shoes, over sporting equipment and gardening tools and coolers and fold-up lawn chairs. Putting his cigarettes in his pocket and making sure he had more matches, he got my mother's old bike, a blue three-speed from Sears with a baby seat. He opened the big garage door, lit another match on his zipper, and tossed it into the gas. The entire garage, because of the open door and the slight breeze, went up in an inferno instantly, lighting up the night a white-yellow.

Michael rode off into the dark morning, with his clock radio and Bible in the baby seat of the bike, his orange cigarette ember a single point of light along the road away from the house.

He felt better already. It had been the right thing to do, the only thing to do. He had left the gas can, with his fingerprints all over it, tipped over in the driveway, the burned matches on the hardwood floor, smoke detectors covered in more fingerprints in trashcans in the house, wires and batteries from the alarms in the pockets of his coat. He went to the end of our road, about a mile away, and sat at the edge of the black river, where wooden fishing boats were tied to pilings, floating on their own dark reflections. He prayed, pulling hard on his third, then his fourth cigarette. He waited for the blue souls of my family to go flying past, toward the safe, bright stars.

EVIDENCE

My father could barely eat, couldn't sleep, days stretched out into absurd, endless things, but then when they were gone he wanted them back, just one more day.

His lungs were filled with fluid and decay. He wheezed, sometimes coughed up blood in the mornings, tossed and turned each night beside my mother, who slept with her face pressed into his back so she could hear his heart. A smattering of BB-sized tumors spread and steadily grew throughout his left lung, emanating from where the one large growth, removed months earlier, had been (though we did not know this at the time).

He was dying quickly; the cancer was in his lymph nodes, poisoning his blood, heading for his liver. He had fevers, headaches, open sores in his throat, the taste of dying in his mouth, and he had lost twenty, then thirty, then forty pounds.

He didn't want to die. He wanted to scream and break things some days because he simply refused for this to continue, but he couldn't muster the strength to do it. He wanted to resist, to put a stop to this, and he began to think of not just this but his entire life as a failed resistance, a battle endlessly lost, over and over, the specifics of each defeat slightly different, sure, but defeat all the same. He was fifty-one, not just dying but obsessed with it, thinking about it all the time, reading about the exact symptoms he was going through in articles and pamphlets given to him by his doctor.

This couldn't be all there was to his life, he thought. Life could not simply be a slew of disappointments, punctuated by moments of happiness, leading toward death. Could it? Could it really be, as he had once heard me say in one of my pedantic early college Eastern philosophical rants, that *all that you suffer is all that you are,* that not extinguishing suffering but in fact coming to terms with it, making sense of it, was the key to the only earthly peace we might ever have? Because if that was the case, fuck it. *Fuck* God.

My father would have sold his soul for just a few more years of life. What was eternity—if there was such a thing— compared to lying beside your beautiful wife while she slept, listening to her breathe, telling your sons all the things you'd always been too uncomfortable and self-conscious to say?

What was eternity compared to fresh air, your health, watching grandchildren toddle around and smile, making love with someone you loved more than anything? Life had slipped away before he could realize how much he wanted it, how much he'd give for a small piece of his future back. He wanted, on his deathbed, to turn into the kind of man who held the ones he loved, who breathed them in, touched them, put his lips against their faces. But how do you change who you are? And what would people think of him?

Once, a few months from this night, when he had become even sicker, my father told me that if we owned a gun, and if Michael hadn't already used it to kill us all, he'd go ahead and put it in his mouth and blow his brains out, as his grandfather had. He could not bear his own death, and at moments he wanted to spread the misery, to share a little of the pain. He wanted to make sure I felt just *some* of what he was feeling. It was only fair. He couldn't take this all alone. No one can be expected to take it all alone.

I remember he spoke to me slowly, clearly enunciating every single word, his voice on the edge of breaking, his eyes filled with tears, with how much he did not mean it. He said he'd walk outside, so I wouldn't have to get rid of the furniture or paint the walls. There's a limit, you know, he said. There has to be a *limit*. Then he stared hard in my face, as if he expected me to say something, to thank him for promising that favor, the favor of not making me clean up the mess of another lost life. But I couldn't speak.

—

The night of the fire had been an exceptionally bad one for my father. Winter nights were hard on his lungs. Earlier he had expectorated blood, bending over the toilet, hacking and coughing until his face went pink and his temples pulsed with the force. My mother stayed in the bathroom with him.

Michael had been stomping through the house, going upstairs to his room, then walking down the stairs heavily, going out the front door, walking around to the garage so he didn't have to walk directly past my family. It was thirty degrees out and he had on only a T-shirt, but my mother noticed sweat dripping off his face, his greasy, unkempt bangs stuck to his forehead.

Later, when my father could sit on the couch, they could hear him praying in the garage, the word "God" cutting through the night. Then he started chanting "Utok Utok Utok." They wondered what he was doing but knew better than to ask. Better to let him be by himself until the next day, when, they hoped, he'd be calmer, closer to rational. Sometimes he'd snap out of it and have a few fairly calm days of TV watching and smoking before the next episode. My mother knew she had to get him to a doctor and get a new prescription of drugs to try. They all knew to lock their doors tonight. My younger brother would turn on a loud fan so he could sleep through all the stomping.

Several hours later my father woke up in bed, wheezing. He couldn't breathe. He sat up. The air was blue, thick. Sick, barely able to move earlier, he got out of bed and shook my mother awake. Pain shot through his side.

Michael's trying to murder us, were the first words out of his mouth, my mother told me. He's trying to kill us.

The fire in the house was out and smoldering. Smoke smudged out the shapes of furniture, doorways. My father coughed. The hardwood floor was treated and fire-resistant. The closed windows kept the flames from spreading to the drapes or furniture, which would have gone up quickly. Once the gasoline burned off, the fire went out, leaving big black circles on the floor. It was the smoke that was dangerous. And the quickly spreading fire in the garage, at the other end of the house, where the large door was wide open and flames billowed out in waves.

My father, in suede slippers and a robe, barely able to move earlier, made his way upstairs, over charred wood and through smoke so thick he couldn't see the walls or his feet or the floor. He banged on Ron's door, but the fan was on and Ron was a heavy sleeper. He banged some more, then kicked the door with the bottom of his burnt left slipper, a nearly miraculous act considering his health, until Ron finally woke up and opened the door.

By 5:40 A.M., my father, mother, and brother were outside, in sweat clothes and robes and slippers and ski coats.

The garage, attached to the house, was lighting up the night in bright flames.

My father, coughing, got the garden hose and began spraying it futilely into the flames, the heat drying out his eyes, making his skin itch. Because of his weak lungs, he would contract pneumonia on this night and die in exactly seven months and twenty-nine days, a good year earlier than his prognosis. So, in a way, my brother got what he wanted.

Within minutes—because of the small size of our town and a call from a neighbor—three police cars, an ambulance, and two fire trucks were parked in front of the house, lights blue and red, circles of color spinning in the darkness.

Neighbors came out to stand with my mother in their nightgowns and pajamas, shivering, asking had what happened, saying how sorry they were, how awful it was, hugging her as she stood in the street, in the darkest part of morning, everyone there knowing it was Michael who had set it.

My father felt dizzy and weak. The EMTs took him to the ambulance. He sat on the bumper, refusing to get in, breathing from an oxygen tank.

By 6:00 A.M., five hours before I returned home from North Carolina to see the damage, my father was talking to Investigator B in muffled tones about what had happened, how it was his twenty-six-year-old schizophrenic son—a really sick kid, *a very sick kid* (still calling him *kid* even now)—the clear oxygen mask steaming up over his mouth and nose, the paramedic telling him to calm down.

My father, that night, told Ron and my mother through wheezes that this was the best thing that could have happened. We're alive, he said, voice muffled through the mask. We could be three charred bodies in there, he said, pointing toward the house. He'll be put away. They'll put him somewhere where they can take care of him. Now they'll have to help . . .

He stopped before he could finish the thought. My father, in that instant, feared Michael might have tried to kill himself, set *himself* on fire. He thought, in fact, that Michael was in the garage right now, writhing around, blazing, skin separating from bone. He started to panic. He told the investigator and the other police officers to go into the garage with the firemen and look for his son. Go in there now, he shouted. He tried to get up, but the EMT held him. His son had tried to murder him, but he was still his son, and he didn't want him to die, not now, not here in the home he'd built.

Just as my father and mother told the police to go in after him, Michael rode up on the soot-covered bike, scribbled-over Bible and alarm clock still in the baby seat. He stopped between the squad car and the ambulance.

The entire scene, the literal end of his life in the free world, had an odd air of the anticlimactic. He sat, one foot on a pedal and one on the ground, and lit a cigarette. He acted as if the house weren't burning, as if there weren't neighbors and cops and an ambulance and fire trucks. He was gone forever, and there was nothing anyone could do about it, and this story, as much as I wish it could, as much as I need it to, cannot change the world as it was, as it is.

The firemen, now inside collecting evidence, were stunned by the incompetence of the arsonist. One of the cops, I'm not sure which one, thumbs wedged between his gunbelt and gut, walked over to Michael, asked him if he wouldn't mind getting in the car for a few questions.

Michael smiled, the tiny metal transistor in his head ticking like flies' legs on glass, a cigarette dangling from his lips. He put out his hands for the handcuffs, turned to my mother, and nonchalantly asked her what she was going to make him for breakfast.

—

From the local section of *The Daily Press,* Wednesday, February 24, 1993:

ANGRY AT FAMILY, MAN SETS FIRE TO HOME FALSELY CONFESSED TO MURDER LAST YEAR

A 26-year-old man who confessed last year to killing a 13-year-old Hampton boy but was cleared by police allegedly set two fires in his house while his parents and brother were asleep, police said Tuesday.

Michael Scott Bottoms of the first block of Rue Degrasse was being held without bond at Central State Hospital in Petersburg Tuesday on three counts of attempted murder and one count of arson, said police Investigator ███ B███████.

Bottoms was sent to the psychiatric hospital for evaluation after the Monday morning incident, ████████ said.

About 5:30 A.M. Monday, Bottoms' father, Ronald, woke up when he smelled smoke outside the master bedroom on the first floor of the two-story house, ████████ said.

He saw smoke in the halls and found a fire in the garage, which is connected to the house, ████████ said. He then got his wife and youngest son and took them outside, ████████ said.

Investigators discovered signs of a splattered liquid at the scene and found that a second fire outside the master bedroom had gone out on its own, ████████ said.

"When a fire's in two locations like that, you know right off the bat it's arson," he said.

Smoke detectors outside the downstairs bedroom and in an upstairs hall had been removed and were found in trash cans inside the house, ████████ said.

Michael Bottoms was not home at the time, ████████ said.

While investigators were at the scene, Michael Bottoms returned home, riding a bicycle, ████████

said. The bicycle had soot on it, suggesting that it had been in the garage when the fire broke out, he said.

Bottoms was taken to police headquarters, where he confessed to the crime and was charged, ████████ said. Bottoms said he had poured gasoline and had started the fire with matches because he was mad at his family, ████████ said.

The fire caused about $10,000 damage, he said.

The family could not be reached for comment Tuesday evening.

Last spring, while he was a resident of the ████ ████ Home for Adults in Newport News, Bottoms called police to confess to the June 10, 1983, murder of 13-year-old ██████████████.

He was held at ██████ State Hospital for observation while Hampton police checked DNA evidence from the original crime scene and matched it with samples from Bottoms' blood.

The test showed Bottoms was not connected to the slaying.

Bottoms said at the time that he confessed to the killing because he wanted to get out of the adult home where he was living.

Nine months later, from *The Daily Press*, Wednesday, November 24, 1993:

POQUOSON MAN SENTENCED TO
30 YEARS FOR SETTING FIRES
GUILTY OF ARSON, ATTEMPTED MURDER

A man who last year falsely confessed to the 1983 murder of a 13-year-old boy was sentenced Tuesday to 30 years in prison for setting two fires in his house while his parents and brother slept.

Michael Scott Bottoms, 26, of the first block of Rue DeGrasse Street, Poquoson, pleaded guilty to three counts of attempted murder and a count of arson for setting the fires Feb. 22.

In court, Bottoms "made a statement to the effect that he never hurt anyone before and he already spent a year in jail and thought it was enough," said Assistant Commonwealth's Attorney Eileen Addison.

Judge Samuel T. Powell handed down the 50-year term, then suspended 20 years. He also recommended that Bottoms serve the sentence at a facility where he would get psychiatric help. . . .

Ronald Bottoms, Sr., has since died and his widow [and two other sons] did not attend Tuesday's hearing. They submitted victim impact statements to the court and Addison said they supported the sentence.

"The father passed away about a month ago, which just leaves his mother and younger brother at home, and his mother is just not able to care for him," Addison said. "He's not getting any better, he's continuing to deteriorate and she's very frightened of him.

"As much as she cares for him and loves him, she's no longer able to care for him at home," the prosecutor added.

APOCRYPHA

Our true stories, as we continually reshape them in the mind, are often the ones that we wish most to forget—a kind of apocrypha from our lives, the things that we keep secret and attempt to excise from the narrative of the self.

For a long time after Michael went to prison, I never spoke his name. When asked, I said I had only one brother, younger. I couldn't say the name "Michael" without feeling sick and anxious and embarrassed and sad. Acknowledging his existence was admitting his link to me and to all my weaknesses, failures, and humiliations. And it was, it is. Because no matter how I might define success, I am equally formed, if not more so, of human failure, mortal inadequacy, of loss as well as gain, and I am part of my brother just as he—whether he knows it or not, whether either of us want it or not—is part of me.

Michael has his own stories, and sometimes, I imagine, I am a character in one of those, a blurry ghost from his past, hovering on the periphery of his dreams. We all have to make sense. And Michael spends his time writing letters in the psychiatric wing of a maximum-security prison, where he is serving his thirty-year sentence, trying to make sense. He used to send them to my mother before she moved away from that house, before I convinced her that she had to move away from there, away from those memories and into a new life.

Michael's letters, in those first years after his incarceration, came on Hallmark cards; the cards had pictures of prairies and blue skies, of young couples holding hands and smiling; they had messages like "Every day is a new beginning" or "Life is what you make it." The envelopes were stamped CORRECTIONAL FACILITY in dark blue ink. Each card was covered in biblical verses—Revelation and Corinthians mostly, his favorites.

Inside, his writing was remarkably clear. He said he was sorry and asked for forgiveness, said that he loved our mother and he loved me and he loved my younger brother Ron. He said that he loved us all, always had and always would, and I believed him, because I don't think any of this happened for lack of love; I think, in fact, that the story of my brother, of my family, could be construed as a story of how wrong love might go, when mental illness—when spirits and angels and demons—invade your life.

Before my father died, he made us promise never to contact Michael again, no matter how we might feel in the future. It was the only way. He didn't succeed in murdering anyone the first time around, he said, and only a fool would give him a second chance. Feel sorry for him from afar. If he comes back into your life, he said, someone is going to die. There was no arguing with that, and we've all found a peace without Michael that we're not willing to give up.

Last year Michael came up for parole. I slept fitfully during the week before his hearing. I couldn't eat, I was petrified. It all seemed as if it were going to happen again. I called my mother every day that week, to see if she had heard anything, to see how she was doing, which was always better than I was, because she is, deep down, a stronger person. Finally, on a Saturday morning, she called to tell me that he had not been given parole, that the person from the parole board whom she had spoken with had said that he was "not doing well, not at all," that he was violent and uncooperative, and that he would most likely have to serve the full length of his sentence.

My mother and I felt a sad sort of relief, yet being confronted with all this again rendered us both speechless. So we just stayed on the line, listening to each other breathe.

Acknowledgments

Thanks to the Virginia Commission for the Arts for the Individual Artist Fellowship that kept me from sinking, the University of the South, Sewanee, for the Tennessee Williams Scholarship, and the University of Virginia for the Henry Hoyns Fellowship and the great library.

Thanks to the writers who helped me along the way: Michael Pearson, Janet Peery, Sheri Reynolds, Ben Marcus, Mark Richard, George Garrett, Deborah Eisenberg, and Doug Day.

Thanks to my wonderful agent Jenny Bent for all of her support and for putting this book into the hands of Doug Pepper, my editor at Crown, who performed wonders.

Thanks to the editors of *Creative Nonfiction* and *Salon,* where a portion of *Angelhead,* in slightly different form, first appeared.

And thanks especially to my wife and mother—the best people I know.

About the Author

Greg Bottoms was born in Hampton, Virginia, in 1970. He received his MFA in fiction from the University of Virginia. His stories and essays have appeared in *Alaska Quarterly Review*, *The Beacon Best of 1999*, *Creative Nonfiction*, *Nerve*, *Prism International*, *Salon*, and elsewhere. He and his wife live in the Shenandoah Valley of Virginia.